LECTIONARY FOR THE CHRISTIAN PEOPLE

LECTIONARY
FOR THE CHRISTIAN PEOPLE

Cycle A of the Roman,
Episcopal, Lutheran Lectionaries

Revised Standard Version texts
emended

PUEBLO PUBLISHING COMPANY

Editors: Gordon Lathrop and Gail Ramshaw-Schmidt

Design: Frank Kacmarcik

Texts from scripture based on the Revised Standard Version of the Bible

Printed in the United States of America

ISBN: 0-916134-79-2

TABLE OF CONTENTS

Episcopal Lectionary

Lutheran Lectionary

INTRODUCTION

It is becoming commonplace for Christian lectors and presiders to emend the translation of the lectionary to eliminate sexist language. Voluminous scholarship attests to this need: we will not take time here to defend this practice. However, all too often those emending the lectionary have no expertise in the biblical languages or do not carefully distinguish between translation and paraphrase. The highly publicized lectionary of the National Council of Churches, *An Inclusive Language Lectionary*, proved too radical for most liturgical use. In order to keep this project within bounds, the decision was made to offer the Sunday readings for the Roman, Episcopal, and Lutheran lectionaries, cycle A, appropriately cross-referenced. As well are included seven of the historic Paschal Vigil lessons and the readings for several significant holy days. It is hoped that other adaptations of the Roman lectionary will profit by using as much of this revision as possible. Unfortunately, the full Consultation on Common Texts (CCT) lectionary could not be served at this time.

The goal of this revision is to provide a translation of the lectionary based on the contemporary American English consensus concerning generic language. This lectionary is basically conservative in its maintenance of key biblical imagery, with the hope that it will be used extensively in average American parishes. Great attention has been given to the sound of the readings, since the lectionary is meant for public proclamation. The following are our general principles for revision:

1. The Revised Standard Version (RSV) has been chosen as the translation on which the revision is based because it is the most trustworthy and ecumenical biblical translation available for speakers of American English. It is an approved translation for Roman Catholics. Many revisions constitute a more faithful rendering of the Hebrew and Greek; others employ an altering of syntax required when translating one language into another. We invite those studying this lectionary to compare it with the original languages.

2. Masculine pronouns for God have been eliminated. At places participial constructions have been used, nouns appropriate to the context supplied, and occasionally sentences cast in the passive voice.

3. The dual rendering for LORD and Lord, as translations of the tetragrammaton and of *Kyrios*, has been retained as the best solution for the present. As well, this keeps the language of the lessons the same as the language of the liturgy.

4. Masculine pronouns for Jesus have been considerably reduced. The Christian conviction that God became incarnate in a particular male human being does allow us use of masculine language for Christ. Following the classical christological understanding, no distinction has been made between Jesus of Nazareth and the risen Christ.

5. In Old Testament passages, which speak of the davidic messiah, which were understood as masculine, and which have been interpreted by Christians as signaling Christ, masculine references have been greatly reduced, but not wholly eliminated. The apocalyptic resonance of the New Testament title *huios tou anthropou*, usually translated "Son of Man," has been suggested by the translation "Man of Heaven."

6. Father and Son language has been retained for trinitarian titles. Jesus is the Son of the Father. When father appears in apposition to God, commas are inserted to distance the word God from the title Father. Jesus' calling of God Father in the gospels has been retained.

7. The *thou* used in the RSV in address to God has been changed to *you*.

8. Masculine designations as generic for humankind have been eliminated. Neither are occupational titles, such as shepherd, assumed to be masculine. Sometimes this results in casting the sentence in the plural, as is common now in American English. It is astounding how often masculine designations have entered the text in English translations and have no basis in the original language.

9. Many biblical passages are inconsistent in grammatical person, that is, alternating between second person plural (you) and third person singular (he). Rendering such passages with a more contemporary consistency, this lectionary uses either the second person plural (you) throughout or the third person plural (they) throughout, thus replacing the third person singular (he).

10. In narrative and parable no attempt has been made to generalize the sex of specific persons or to include persons of the opposite sex in a desire for balance. The original images of the story have been retained.

11. Greek narrative can refer to a specific named individual with a participial construction or within a verbal form in a way that English cannot. Contemporary usage suggests that at times "a man" or "a woman" be inserted.

12. Some lessons contain poetic formulations in which sexuality is ascribed to nongender-specific things or beings. In sustained conceits, as in the Lady Wisdom poems, the sexual imagery is retained. In isolated verses, as in reference to a city as *she* or to an angel as *he*, since contemporary English does not have grammatical gender, the sexual references are eliminated.

13. When translating the biblical source of common liturgical texts, as in the opening lines of the Gloria in excelsis in Luke 2, the attempt has been made to cast the translation in its most familiar contemporary liturgical form. Thus there are echoes of the ICEL translations in this lectionary.

14. When a passage is extremely familiar, an attempt has been made to recast the syntax so that the revision does not sound like a mistake.

15. Because there is diversity among the churches in the way readings are begun, this lectionary has provided only such lead-in phrases (*incipits*) as are necessary for understanding. These lead-in phrases are drawn from the context and are in brackets. In certain gospel readings, we have added the traditional "at that time."

16. Proper names replace pronoun references in narratives to reduce "he" and to assist aural comprehension.

17. Some lessons, pp. 17, 18, and 250, are essentially sexist in speaking specifically of a subordinate position of women. Such problematic lessons are translated faithful to the original, with the hope that future lectionary revisions will choose other readings as more appropriate for today's church. Such lessons are marked with a §.

18. The following are examples of recurring alterations:

king, in reference to God = Sovereign
king, in reference to Jesus or messiah = king usually retained
king, in reference to humankind = ruler, unless a named king
kingdom of God = dominion of God
kingdom on earth = realm or country or kingdom
God our Father = God, our Father
father, in Hebrew image for God = "as father"
fathers, as in ancestors = forebears
men of X, in direct address = O Xeans
sons, as generic term = children
God himself = that very God
by his mercy = out of mercy, God
Son of Man = Man of Heaven
he who = the one who, those who
brethren, in direct address = my dear people
brethren, in reference to group = the community or similar
     phrase
fellowship = communion
member, of human body = physical part
babe = infant
in travail = in labor pangs
the circumcized = the Jewish people
the Jews = depending on context: the Judeans, the Jewish
     people, the Jews
anthropos, anthropon = depending on context: mortals, human
     beings, person, humankind, a man, others, people,
     everyone, those

However, euphony or specific context may have led to a different decision in revision.

Translation always requires choices between subtleties. In order to gain inclusiveness we have pluralized texts ("he" becomes "they") and have thereby sometimes diminished directness. Replacing "his people" with "the people of God" may seem to create distance. A few words cannot say all the truth at once.

Unfortunately, we have not been able to include revisions of the psalm for the day. Several inclusive language translations of the psalms are available: *Consultation on a Liturgical Psalter* (Washington, DC: International Commission on English in the Liturgy, 1984) and Gary Chamberlain's *The Psalms: A New Translation for Prayer and Worship* (Nashville: The Upper Room, 1984).

We hope that this lectionary will prove of service to the liturgical assemblies of our lands.

Gordon W. Lathrop
Gail Ramshaw-Schmidt

A GUIDE TO THE USE OF THE LECTIONARY

Find the Sunday or Feast Day according to the title used in:

R—the Roman Catholic lectionary and sacramentary
E—the American Episcopalian *Book of Common Prayer*
L—the *Lutheran Book of Worship*

Find the reading to be proclaimed. The chapter and verses indicated in the official liturgical books are listed and are also marked

R—the Roman Catholic lectionary according to the *Editio Typica*, second edition
E—the lectionary of the *Book of Common Prayer*
L—the lectionary of the *Lutheran Book of Worship*

Note that when two or more official lectionaries agree on the reading, even partially, the full biblical passage involved is printed only once.

Identify the verses in the printed passage that are proper to your community's lectionary. Verse numbers are included in the printed passage only where necessary to identify beginnings, endings, and omitted passages. If verses are to be omitted, readers will have to be attentive to sentence structure, supplying missing words from the context. The difference between Latin syntax and the English of this translation suggests that sometimes more verses and fuller sentences should be proclaimed than are called for in the *Editio Typica*. Note that occasionally the Latin versification of the Roman lectionary differs from the numbering found in English language translations. That difference has been noted.

Supply the reading with the introductory words and concluding phrases proper to your community's use.

Note further:

• Seven readings for the Vigil of Easter have been included. They are printed in the longest and most inclusive form in which they appear in any of the lectionaries. They have not been marked according to denominational use, but together they provide a sufficient selection to meet the requirements of all three sets of liturgical books.

• The sign § is used to mark readings currently included in the official lectionaries in which the essential problems of inclusivity and sexism cannot be resolved by translation or responsible linguistic emendation.

R E L   FIRST SUNDAY OF ADVENT

FIRST READING

R E L   Isaiah 2:1–5

[1]The word which Isaiah the son of Amoz saw concerning Judah
and Jerusalem.
It shall come to pass in the latter days
    that the mountain of the house of the LORD
shall be established as the highest of the mountains,
    and shall be raised above the hills;
and all the nations shall flow to it,
    and many peoples shall come, and say:
"Come, let us go up to the mountain of the LORD,
    to the house of Jacob's God,
who will teach us the ways of the LORD,
    that we may walk in the paths of God."
For out of Zion shall go forth the law,
    and the word of the LORD from Jerusalem.
God shall judge between the nations,
    and shall decide for many peoples;
and they shall beat their swords into plowshares,
    and their spears into pruning hooks;
nation shall not lift up sword against nation,
    neither shall they learn war any more.
[5]O house of Jacob,
    come, let us walk
    in the light of the LORD.

SECOND READING

R L   Romans 13:11–14a
E   Romans 13:8–14

[8]Owe no one anything, except to love one another; for those
who love their neighbors have fulfilled the law. The commandments, "You shall not commit adultery, You shall not kill, You
shall not steal, You shall not covet," and any other commandment, are summed up in this sentence, "You shall love your
neighbor as yourself." Love does no wrong to a neighbor;
therefore love is the fulfilling of the law.

[11]"Besides this you know what hour it is, how it is full time now for you to wake from sleep. For salvation is nearer to us now than when we first believed; the night is far gone, the day is at hand. Let us then cast off the works of darkness and put on the armor of light; let us conduct ourselves becomingly as in the day, not in reveling and drunkenness, not in debauchery and licentiousness, not in quarreling and jealousy. [14a]But put on the Lord Jesus Christ, [14b]and make no provision for the flesh, to gratify its desires.

GOSPEL

R E L   Matthew 24:37–44

[At that time Jesus said,]

[37]"As were the days of Noah, so will be the coming of the Man of Heaven. For as in those days before the flood they were eating and drinking, marrying and giving in marriage, until the day when Noah entered the ark, and they did not know until the flood came and swept them all away, so will be the coming of the Man of Heaven. Then two men will be in the field; one is taken and one is left. Two women will be grinding at the mill; one is taken and one is left. Watch therefore, for you do not know on what day your Lord is coming. But be sure of this: knowing in what part of the night the thief was coming, the owner of the house would have watched and would not have let the house be broken into. [44]Therefore you also must be ready; for the Man of Heaven is coming at an hour you do not expect."

FIRST READING

R E L   Isaiah 11:1–10

¹There shall come forth a shoot from the stump of Jesse,
   and a branch shall grow out of its roots.
Upon this one the Spirit of the LORD shall rest,
   the spirit of wisdom and understanding,
   the spirit of counsel and might,
   the spirit of knowledge and the fear of the LORD.
And his delight shall be in the fear of the LORD.
He shall not judge by what the eyes see,
   or decide by what the ears hear;
but with righteousness he shall judge the poor,
   and decide with equity for the meek of the earth;
and he shall smite the earth with the rod of his mouth,
   and with the breath of his lips shall slay the wicked.
Righteousness shall be the belt of his waist,
   and faithfulness shall gird his loins.
The wolf shall dwell with the lamb,
   and the leopard shall lie down with the kid,
and the calf and the lion and the fatling together,
   and a little child shall lead them.
The cow and the bear shall feed;
   their young shall lie down together;
   and the lion shall eat straw like the ox.
The sucking child shall play over the hole of the asp,
   and the weaned child shall put a hand on the adder's den.
They shall not hurt or destroy
   in all my holy mountain;
for the earth shall be full of the knowledge of the LORD
   as the waters cover the sea.

¹⁰In that day there will stand as an ensign to the peoples the root of Jesse, whom the nations shall seek, and whose dwellings shall be glorious.

SECOND READING

R   Romans 15:4–9

E   L   Romans 15:4–13

[4]Whatever was written in former days was written for our instruction, that by steadfastness and by the encouragement of the scriptures we might have hope. May the God of steadfastness and encouragement grant you to live in such harmony with one another, in accord with Christ Jesus, that together you may with one voice glorify the God and Father of our Lord Jesus Christ.

Welcome one another, therefore, as Christ has welcomed you, for the glory of God. For I tell you that Christ became a servant to the Jewish people to show God's truthfulness, in order that the promises given to the forebears be confirmed, [9]and in order that the Gentiles might glorify God because of mercy. As it is written,

"Therefore I will praise you among the Gentiles,
and sing to your name";

[10]and again it is said,

"Rejoice, O Gentiles, with the people of God";

and again,

"Praise the Lord, all Gentiles;
let all peoples praise the Lord";

and further Isaiah says,

"There shall come the root of Jesse,
who rises to rule the Gentiles,
in whom the Gentiles shall hope"

[13]May the God of hope fill you with all joy and peace in believing, so that by the power of the Holy Spirit you may abound in hope.

GOSPEL

R E L Matthew 3:1–12

¹In those days came John the Baptist, preaching in the wilderness of Judea, "Repent, for the dominion of heaven is at hand." For this is the one who was spoken of by the prophet Isaiah who said,

"The voice of one crying in the wilderness:
Prepare the way of the Lord;
make straight the paths of the Lord."

Now John wore a garment of camel's hair, and a leather belt around his waist; and his food was locusts and wild honey. Then went out to him Jerusalem and all Judea and all the region about the Jordan, and they were baptized by him in the river Jordan, confessing their sins.

But when John saw many of the Pharisees and Sadducees coming for baptism, he said to them, "You brood of vipers! Who warned you to flee from the wrath to come? Bear fruit that befits repentance, and do not presume to say to yourselves, 'We have Abraham as our father'; for I tell you, God is able from these stones to raise up children to Abraham. Even now the axe is laid to the root of the trees; every tree therefore that does not bear good fruit is cut down and thrown into the fire.

"I baptize you with water for repentance, but the one who is coming after me, the one mightier than I, whose sandals I am not worthy to carry, will baptize you with the Holy Spirit and with fire. ¹²With a winnowing fork in hand, the mighty one will clear the threshing floor and gather the wheat into the granary, burning the chaff with unquenchable fire."

FIRST READING

R   Isaiah 35:1–6a, 10
E L Isaiah 35:1–10

¹The wilderness and the dry land shall be glad,
    the desert shall rejoice and blossom;
like the crocus it shall blossom abundantly,
    and rejoice with joy and singing.
The glory of Lebanon shall be given to it,
    the majesty of Carmel and Sharon.
They shall see the glory of the LORD,
    the majesty of our God.
Strengthen the weak hands,
    and make firm the feeble knees.
Say to those who are of a fearful heart,
    "Be strong, fear not!
Behold, your God
    will come with vengeance,
with the recompense of God.
    God will come and save you."
Then the eyes of the blind shall be opened,
    and the ears of the deaf unstopped;
⁶ᵃthen shall the lame leap like a hart,
    and the tongue of the dumb sing for joy.
⁶ᵇFor the waters shall break forth in the wilderness,
    and streams in the desert;
the burning sand shall become a pool,
    and the thirsty ground springs of water;
the haunt of jackals shall become a swamp,
    the grass shall become reeds and rushes.
And a highway shall be there,
    and it shall be called the Holy Way;
the unclean shall not pass over it,
    and fools shall not err therein.
No lion shall be there,
    nor shall any ravenous beast come up on it;

they shall not be found there,
  but the redeemed shall walk there.
¹⁰And the ransomed of the Lord shall return,
  and come to Zion with singing;
  everlasting joy shall be upon their heads;
  they shall obtain joy and gladness,
  and sorrow and sighing shall flee away.

SECOND READING

R E L   James 5:7–10

⁷Be patient, therefore, my dear people, until the coming of the Lord. Behold, the farmer waits for the precious fruit of the earth, being patient over it until it receives the early and the late rain. You also be patient. Establish your hearts, for the coming of the Lord is at hand. Do not grumble, dear people, against one another, that you may not be judged; behold, the Judge is standing at the doors. ¹⁰As an example of suffering and patience, my dear ones, take the prophets who spoke in the name of the Lord.

GOSPEL

R E L   Matthew 11:2–11

²Now John, hearing in prison about the deeds of the Christ, sent word by his disciples and said to Jesus, "Are you the one who is to come, or shall we look for another?" And Jesus answered them, "Go and tell John what you hear and see: the blind receive their sight and the lame walk, lepers are cleansed and the deaf hear, and the dead are raised up, and the poor have good news preached to them. And blessed are they who take no offense at me."

As they went away, Jesus began to speak to the crowds concerning John: "What did you go out into the wilderness to behold? A reed shaken by the wind? Why then did you go out? To see someone clothed in soft raiment? Behold, those who wear soft raiment are in palaces. Why then did you go out? To see a prophet? Yes, I tell you, and more than a prophet. This is the one of whom it is written,

'Behold, I send my messenger before your face,
who shall prepare your way before you.'

[11]"Truly, I say to you, among those born of women there has
risen no one greater than John the Baptist; yet whoever is least
in the dominion of heaven is greater than he."

FIRST READING

R L   Isaiah 7:10–14
   E   Isaiah 7:10–17

¹⁰Again the LORD spoke to Ahaz, "Ask a sign of the LORD your God; let it be deep as Sheol or high as heaven." But Ahaz said, "I will not ask, and I will not put the LORD to the test." And the LORD said, "Hear then, O house of David! Is it too little for you to weary humankind, that you weary my God also? ¹⁴Therefore this very Lord will give you a sign. Behold, a young woman shall conceive and bear a son, and shall call his name Immanuel. ¹⁵He shall eat curds and honey when he knows how to refuse the evil and choose the good. For before the child knows how to refuse the evil and choose the good, the land before whose two kings you are in dread will be deserted. ¹⁷The LORD will bring upon you and upon your people and upon your dynasty such days as have not come since the day that Ephraim departed from Judah."

SECOND READING

R E L   Romans 1:1–7

¹Paul, a servant of Jesus Christ, called to be an apostle, set apart for the gospel of God which God promised beforehand through prophets in the holy scriptures, the gospel concerning God's Son, who was descended from David according to the flesh and designated Son of God in power according to the Spirit of holiness by the resurrection from the dead, Jesus Christ our Lord, through whom we have received grace and apostleship to bring about the obedience of faith for the sake of the Lord's name among all the nations, including yourselves who are called to belong to Jesus Christ;

⁷To all God's beloved in Rome, who are called to be saints:

Grace to you and peace from God, our Father, and the Lord
   Jesus Christ.

GOSPEL

R   Matthew 1:18–24
E   L   Matthew 1:18–25

[18]Now the birth of Jesus Christ took place in this way. When his mother Mary had been betrothed to Joseph, before they came together she was found to be with child of the Holy Spirit; and her husband Joseph, being just, and unwilling to put her to shame, resolved to divorce her quietly. But as he considered this, behold, an angel of the Lord appeared to him in a dream, saying, "Joseph, son of David, do not fear to take Mary your wife, for that which is conceived in her is of the Holy Spirit; she will bear a son, and you shall call his name Jesus, for he will save his people from their sins." All this took place to fulfill what the Lord had spoken by the prophet:

"Behold, a virgin shall conceive and bear a son,
and his name shall be called Emmanuel"

(which means, God with us). [24]When Joseph woke from sleep, he did as the angel of the Lord commanded him; he took Mary as his wife, [25]but knew her not until she had borne a son; and he called his name Jesus.

R CHRISTMAS MASS AT MIDNIGHT
E CHRISTMAS DAY I
L THE NATIVITY OF OUR LORD, MIDNIGHT

FIRST READING

R L Isaiah 9:2–7
E Isaiah 9:2–4, 6–7

²The people who walked in darkness
  have seen a great light;
those who dwelt in a land of deep darkness,
  on them has light shined.
You have multiplied the nation,
  you have increased its joy;
they rejoice before you
  as with joy at the harvest,
  as they rejoice when dividing spoil.
⁴For the yoke of their burden,
  and the staff of their shoulders,
  the rod of their oppressor,
  you have broken as on the day of Midian.
⁵For every boot of the tramping warrior in battle tumult
  and every garment rolled in blood
  will be burned as fuel for the fire.
⁶For to us a child is born,
  to us a son is given;
and the government will be upon his shoulder,
  and his name will be called
"Wonderful Counselor, Mighty God,
  Everlasting Father, Prince of Peace."
⁷Of the greatness of his government and of peace
  there will be no end,
upon the throne and dominion of David,
  to establish it, and to uphold it
with justice and with righteousness
  from this time forth and for evermore.
The zeal of the LORD of hosts will do this.

R E L Titus 2:11–14

¹¹The grace of God has appeared for the salvation of all people, training us to renounce irreligion and worldly passions, and to live sober, upright, and godly lives in this world, awaiting our blessed hope, the appearing of the glory of the great God and our Savior Jesus Christ, ¹⁴who gave himself for us to redeem us from all iniquity and to purify for himself a chosen people who are zealous for good deeds.

GOSPEL

R E Luke 2:1–14
L Luke 2:1–20

¹In those days a decree went out from Caesar Augustus that all the world should be enrolled. This was the first enrollment, when Quirinius was governor of Syria. And all went to their own city to be enrolled. And Joseph also went up from Galilee, from the city of Nazareth, to Judea, to the city of David, which is called Bethlehem, because he was of the house and lineage of David, to be enrolled with Mary, his betrothed, who was with child. And while they were there, the time came for her to deliver. And she gave birth to her first-born son and wrapped him in swaddling cloths, and laid him in a manger, because there was no place for them in the inn.

And in that region there were shepherds out in the field, keeping watch over their flock by night. And an angel of the Lord appeared to them, and the glory of the Lord shone around them, and they were filled with fear. And the angel said to them, "Be not afraid; for behold, I bring you good news of a great joy which will come to all the people; for to you is born this day in the city of David a Savior, who is Christ the Lord. And this will be a sign for you: you will find an infant wrapped in swaddling cloths and lying in a manger." And suddenly there was with the angel a multitude of the heavenly host praising God and saying,

¹⁴"Glory to God in the highest,
and peace to God's people on earth."

[15]And when the angels went away from them into heaven, the shepherds said to one another, "Let us go over to Bethlehem and see this thing that has happened, which the Lord has made known to us." And they went with haste, and found Mary and Joseph, and the infant lying in a manger. And when they saw it they made known the saying which had been told them concerning this child; and all who heard it wondered at what the shepherds told them. But Mary kept all these things, pondering them in her heart. [20]And the shepherds returned, glorifying and praising God for all they had heard and seen, as it had been told them.

R   CHRISTMAS MASS DURING THE DAY
E   CHRISTMAS DAY III
L   THE NATIVITY OF OUR LORD, MORNING

FIRST READING

R E L   Isaiah 52:7–10

⁷How beautiful upon the mountains
   are the feet of the messenger,
who publishes peace, who brings good tidings of good,
   who publishes salvation,
   who says to Zion, "Your God reigns."
Hark, your sentries lift up their voice,
   together they sing for joy;
for with their own eyes they see
   the return of the LORD to Zion.
Break forth together into singing,
   you waste places of Jerusalem;
for the LORD has comforted the people
   and has redeemed Jerusalem.
¹⁰The holy arm of the LORD is bared
   before the eyes of all nations,
and all the ends of the earth shall see
   the salvation of our God.

SECOND READING

R   Hebrews 1:1–6
E   Hebrews 1:1–12
L   Hebrews 1:1–9

¹In many and various ways God spoke of old to our forebears
by the prophets; but in these last days God has spoken to us
by the Son, whom God appointed the heir of all things, and
through whom God also created the world. This Son reflects
the glory of God and bears the very stamp of God's nature,
upholding the universe by a word of power. The Son, having
made purification for sins, sat down at the right hand of the
Majesty on high, having become as much superior to angels as
the name the Son has obtained is more excellent than theirs.

For to what angel did God ever say,

"You are my Son,
today I have begotten you"?

Or again,

"I will be to him as father,
and he shall be to me as son"?

⁶And again, bringing the first-born into the world, God says,

"Let all God's angels worship him."

⁷Of the angels God says,

"God makes the angels winds,
God's servants flames of fire."

But of the Son God says,

"Your throne, O God, is for ever and ever,
the righteous scepter is the scepter of your dominion.
⁹You have loved righteousness and hated lawlessness;
therefore God, your God, has anointed you
with the oil of gladness beyond your comrades."
¹⁰And,
"You, Lord, founded the earth in the beginning,
and the heavens are the work of your hands;
they will perish, but you remain;
they will all grow old like a garment,
¹²like a mantle you will roll them up,
and they will be changed.
But you are the same,
and your years will never end."

GOSPEL

R   John 1:1–18
E L   John 1:1–14

¹In the beginning was the Word, and the Word was with God,
and the Word was God. The Word was in the beginning with
God; all things were made through the Word, without whom
nothing that was made was made. In the Word was life, and

the life was the light of all. The light shines in the darkness, and the darkness has not overcome it.

There was sent by God a person named John. He came for testimony, to bear witness to the light, that all might believe through him. He was not the light, but came to bear witness to the light.

The true light that enlightens everyone was coming into the world. The light was in the world, and the world was made through the light, yet the world knew him not. He came to his own home, and his own people received him not. But to all who received him, who believed in his name, he gave power to become children of God; who were born, not of blood nor of the will of the flesh nor of the desire of a man, but of God.

[14]And the Word became flesh and dwelt among us, full of grace and truth; we have beheld his glory, glory as of the only Son from the Father. [15](John bore witness to the Word, and cried, "This is the one of whom I said, 'The one who comes after me ranks before me, for he was before me.'") And from the Son's fullness have we all received, grace upon grace. For the law was given through Moses; grace and truth came through Jesus Christ. [18]No one has ever seen God; the only Son, who is in the bosom of the Father, has made God known.

FIRST READING

R Sirach 3:2–6, 12–14 §

> [2]For the Lord honored the father above the children,
>   and confirmed the right of the mother over her sons.
> Honoring one's father atones for sins,
>   and glorifying one's mother is like laying up treasure.
> Those who honor their father will be gladdened by their own
>   children,
>   and when they pray they will be heard.
> [6]Those who glorify their father will have long life,
>   and those who obey the Lord will refresh their mother.
> [12]O child, help your father in his old age,
>   and do not grieve him as long as he lives;
> even if he is lacking in understanding, show forbearance;
>   in all your strength do not despise him.
> [14]For kindness to a father will not be forgotten,
>   and against your sins it will be credited to you.

E Isaiah 61:10–62:3

> [10]I will greatly rejoice in the LORD,
>   my soul shall exult in my God;
> for God has clothed me with the garments of salvation,
>   and covered me with the robe of righteousness,
> as a bridegroom decks himself with a garland,
>   and as a bride adorns herself with her jewels.
> For as the earth brings forth its shoots,
>   and as a garden causes what is sown in it to spring up,
> so the Lord GOD will cause righteousness and praise
>   to spring forth before all the nations.
> For Zion's sake I will not keep silent,
>   and for Jerusalem's sake I will not rest,
> until its vindication goes forth as brightness
>   and its salvation as a burning torch.
> The nations shall see your vindication,
>   and all the rulers your glory;

and you shall be called by a new name
  which the mouth of the LORD will give.
³You shall be a crown of beauty in the hand of the LORD,
  and a royal diadem in the hand of your God.

L   Isaiah 63:7–9

⁷I will recount the steadfast love of the LORD,
  the praises of the LORD,
according to all that the LORD has granted us,
  and the great goodness to the house of Israel
which the LORD has granted them out of mercy,
  out of abundant steadfast love.
For the LORD said, Surely they are my people,
  children who will not deal falsely;
  and the LORD became their Savior.
⁹In all their affliction the LORD was afflicted,
  and the angel of the LORD's presence saved them;
out of love and pity the LORD redeemed them,
  lifting them up and carrying them all the days of old.

SECOND READING

R   Colossians 3:12–21   §

¹²Put on then, as God's chosen ones, holy and beloved, compassion, kindness, lowliness, meekness, and patience, forbear-
ing one another and, if one has a complaint against another,
forgiving each another; as the Lord has forgiven you, so you
also must forgive. And above all these put on love, which
binds everything together in perfect harmony. And let the
peace of Christ rule in your hearts, to which indeed you were
called in the one body. And be thankful. Let the word of Christ
dwell in you richly, teach and admonish one another in all wisdom, and sing psalms and hymns and spiritual songs with
thankfulness in your hearts to God. And whatever you do, in
word or deed, do everything in the name of the Lord Jesus,
giving thanks to God, the Father, through him.

Wives, be subject to your husbands, as is fitting in the Lord.
Husbands, love your wives, and do not be harsh with them.
Children, obey your parents in everything, for this pleases the

Lord. ²¹Parents, do not provoke your children, lest they become discouraged.

E   Galatians 3:23–25, 4:4–7
L   Galatians 4:4–7

²³Now before faith came, we were confined under the law, kept under restraint until faith should be revealed. So that the law was our custodian until Christ came, that we might be justified by faith. ²⁵But now that faith has come, we are no longer under a custodian.

⁴When the time had fully come, God sent forth the Son, born of woman, born under the law, to redeem those who were under the law, so that we might receive adoption. And because you are adopted children, God has sent the Spirit of the Son into our hearts, crying, "Abba! Father!" ⁷So through God you are no longer a slave but an adopted child, and if a child then an heir.

GOSPEL

R L   Matthew 2:13–15, 19–23

¹³Now when the magi had departed, behold, an angel of the Lord appeared to Joseph in a dream and said, "Rise, take the child and his mother, and flee to Egypt, and remain there till I tell you; for Herod is about to search for the child, to destroy him." And Joseph rose and took the child and his mother by night, and departed to Egypt, ¹⁵and remained there until the death of Herod. This was to fulfill what the Lord had spoken by the prophet, "Out of Egypt have I called my son."

¹⁹But when Herod died, behold, an angel of the Lord appeared in a dream to Joseph in Egypt, saying, "Rise, take the child and his mother, and go to the land of Israel, for those who sought the child's life are dead." And Joseph rose and took the child and his mother, and went to the land of Israel. But when he heard that Archelaus reigned over Judea in place of his father Herod, he was afraid to go there, and being warned in a dream he withdrew to the district of Galilee. ²³And he went and dwelt in a city called Nazareth, that what was spoken by the prophets might be fulfilled, "He shall be called a Nazarene."

E   John 1:1–18

¹In the beginning was the Word, and the Word was with God, and the Word was God. The Word was in the beginning with God; all things were made through the Word, without whom nothing that was made was made. In the Word was life, and the life was the light of all. The light shines in the darkness, and the darkness has not overcome it.

There was sent by God a person named John. He came for testimony, to bear witness to the light, that all might believe through him. He was not the light, but came to bear witness to the light.

The true light that enlightens everyone was coming into the world. The light was in the world, and the world was made through the light yet the world knew him not. He came to his own home, and his own people received him not. But to all who received him, who believed in his name, he gave power to become children of God; who were born, not of blood nor of the will of the flesh nor of the desire of a man, but of God.

And the Word became flesh and dwelt among us, full of grace and truth; we have beheld his glory, glory as of the only Son from the Father. (John bore witness to the Word, and cried, "This is the one of whom I said, 'The one who comes after me ranks before me, for he was before me.' ") And from the Son's fullness have we all received, grace upon grace. For the law was given through Moses; grace and truth came through Jesus Christ. ¹⁸No one has ever seen God; the only Son, who is in the bosom of the Father, has made God known.

January 1

R MARY, MOTHER OF GOD
E HOLY NAME
L NAME OF JESUS

FIRST READING

R L Numbers 6:22–27

²²The Lord said to Moses, "Say to Aaron and his sons, Thus you shall bless the people of Israel: you shall say to them,

The Lord bless you and keep you:
The Lord's face shine upon you, and be gracious to you:
The Lord look upon you with favor, and give you peace.

²⁷"So shall they put my name upon the people of Israel, and I will bless them."

E Exodus 34:1–8

¹The Lord said to Moses, "Cut two tables of stone like the first; and I will write upon the tables the words that were on the first tables, which you broke. Be ready in the morning, and come up in the morning to Mount Sinai, and present yourself there to me on the top of the mountain. No one shall come up with you, and let no one be seen throughout all the mountain; let no flocks or herds feed before that mountain." So Moses cut two tables of stone like the first; and he rose early in the morning and went up on Mount Sinai, as the Lord had commanded him, and took in his hand two tables of stone. And the Lord descended in the cloud and stood with him there, and proclaimed the name of the Lord. The Lord passed before Moses, and proclaimed, "The Lord, the Lord, a God merciful and gracious, slow to anger, and abounding in steadfast love and faithfulness, keeping steadfast love for thousands, forgiving iniquity and transgression and sin, but who will by no means clear the guilty, visiting the iniquity of the parents upon the children and the children's children, to the third and the fourth generation." ⁸And Moses made haste to bow his head toward the earth, and worshiped.

SECOND READING

R Galatians 4:4–7

[4]When the time had fully come, God sent forth the Son, born of woman, born under the law, to redeem those who were under the law, so that we might receive adoption. And because you are adopted children, God has sent the Spirit of the Son into our hearts, crying, "Abba! Father!" [7]So through God you are no longer a slave but an adopted child, and if a child then an heir.

E L Romans 1:1–7

[1]Paul, a servant of Jesus Christ, called to be an apostle, set apart for the gospel of God which God promised beforehand through prophets in the holy scriptures, the gospel concerning God's Son, who was descended from David according to the flesh and was designated Son of God in power according to the Spirit of holiness by the resurrection from the dead, Jesus Christ our Lord, through whom we have received grace and apostleship to bring about the obedience of faith for the sake of the Lord's name among all the nations, including yourselves who are called to belong to Jesus Christ;

[7]To all God's beloved in Rome, who are called to be saints:

Grace to you and peace from God, our Father, and the Lord Jesus Christ.

GOSPEL

R Luke 2:16–21
E Luke 2:15–21
L Luke 2:21

[15]And when the angels went away from them into heaven, the shepherds said to one another, "Let us go over to Bethlehem and see this thing that has happened, which the Lord has made known to us." [16]And they went with haste, and found Mary and Joseph, and the baby lying in a manger. And when they saw it they made known the saying which had been told them concerning this child; and all who heard it wondered at what the shepherds told them. But Mary kept all these things,

pondering them in her heart. And the shepherds returned, glorifying and praising God for all they had heard and seen, as it had been told them.

[21]And at the end of eight days, when the child was circumcised, he was called Jesus, the name given by the angel before he was conceived in the womb.

FIRST READING

R   Sirach 24:1–2, 8–12

¹Wisdom will praise herself,
    and will glory in the midst of her people.
²In the assembly of the Most High she will open her mouth,
    and in the presence of God's host she will glory:
⁸"The Creator of all things gave me a commandment,
    and the one who created me assigned a place for my tent,
Saying, 'Make your dwelling in Jacob,
    and in Israel receive your inheritance.'
From eternity, in the beginning, the Most High created me,
    and for eternity I shall not cease to exist.
In the holy tabernacle I ministered before the Most High,
    and so I was established in Zion.
In the beloved city likewise I received a resting place,
    and in Jerusalem was my dominion.
¹²So I took root in an honored people,
    in the portion of the Lord, who is their inheritance."

E   Jeremiah 31:7–14

⁷For thus says the LORD:
"Sing aloud with gladness for Jacob,
    and raise shouts for the chief of the nations;
proclaim, give praise, and say,
    'The LORD has saved the remnant of Israel, the people of the
        LORD.'
Behold, I will bring them from the north country,
    and gather them from the farthest parts of the earth,
among them the blind and the lame,
    the woman with child and her who is in labor, together;
    a great company, they shall return here.
With weeping they shall come,
    and with consolations I will lead them back,
I will make them walk by brooks of water,
    in a straight path in which they shall not stumble;
for I am as a father to Israel,
    and Ephraim is as my first-born.

Hear the word of the LORD, O nations,
and declare it in the coastlands afar off;
say, 'The one who scattered Israel's people will gather them
and will keep them as a shepherd keeps the flock.'
For the LORD has ransomed Jacob,
and has redeemed Jacob from hands too strong for them.
They shall come and sing aloud on the height of Zion,
and they shall be radiant over the goodness of the LORD,
over the grain, the wine, and the oil,
and over the young of the flock and the herd;
their life shall be like a watered garden,
and they shall languish no more.
Then shall the maidens rejoice in the dance,
and the young men and the old shall be merry.
I will turn their mourning into joy,
I will comfort them, and give them gladness for sorrow.
¹⁴I will feast the soul of the priests with abundance,
and my people shall be satisfied with my goodness,
says the LORD."

L   Isaiah 61:10–62:3

¹⁰I will greatly rejoice in the LORD,
my soul shall exult in my God;
for God has clothed me with the garments of salvation,
and covered me with the robe of righteousness,
as a bridegroom decks himself with a garland,
and as a bride adorns herself with her jewels.
For as the earth brings forth its shoots,
and as a garden causes what is sown in it to spring up,
so the Lord GOD will cause righteousness and praise
to spring forth before all the nations.
For Zion's sake I will not keep silent,
and for Jerusalem's sake I will not rest,
until its vindication goes forth as brightness
and its salvation as a burning torch.
The nations shall see your vindication,
and all the rulers your glory;
and you shall be called by a new name
which the mouth of the LORD will give.

³You shall be a crown of beauty in the hand of the LORD,
   and a royal diadem in the hand of your God.

SECOND READING

R L Ephesians 1:3–6, 15–18
  E Ephesians 1:3–6, 15–19a

³Blessed be the God and Father of our Lord Jesus Christ, who
has blessed us in Christ with every spiritual blessing in the
heavenly places, even as God chose us in Christ before the
foundation of the world, that before God we should be holy
and blameless. God destined us in love for adoption through
Jesus Christ: this was God's good pleasure and will, ⁶to the
praise of God's glorious grace freely bestowed on us in the
Beloved.

¹⁵For this reason, because I have heard of your faith in the Lord
Jesus and your love toward all the saints, I do not cease to give
thanks for you, remembering you in my prayers, that the God
of our Lord Jesus Christ, the Father of glory, may give you a
spirit of wisdom and of revelation, that you may know God,
¹⁸having the eyes of your hearts enlightened, that you may
know what is the hope to which God has called you, what are
the riches of God's glorious inheritance in the saints, ¹⁹ᵃand
what is the immeasurable greatness of God's power in us who
believe.

GOSPEL

R L John 1:1–18

¹In the beginning was the Word, and the Word was with God,
and the Word was God. The Word was in the beginning with
God; all things were made through the Word, without whom
nothing that was made was made. In the Word was life, and
the life was the light of all. The light shines in the darkness,
and the darkness has not overcome it.

There was sent by God a person named John. He came for
testimony, to bear witness to the light, that all might believe
through him. He was not the light, but came to bear witness to
the light.

The true light that enlightens everyone was coming into the world. The light was in the world, and the world was made through the light, yet the world knew him not. He came to his own home, and his own people received him not. But to all who received him, who believed in his name, he gave power to become children of God; who were born, not of blood nor of the will of the flesh nor of the desire of a man, but of God.

And the Word became flesh and dwelt among us, full of grace and truth; we have beheld his glory, glory as of the only Son from the Father. (John bore witness to the Word, and cried, "This is the one of whom I said, 'The one who comes after me ranks before me, for he was before me.'") And from the Son's fullness have we all received, grace upon grace. For the law was given through Moses; grace and truth came through Jesus Christ. [18]No one has ever seen God; the only Son, who is in the bosom of the Father, has made God known.

E   Matthew 2:13–15, 19–23

[13]Now when the magi had departed, behold, an angel of the Lord appeared to Joseph in a dream and said, "Rise, take the child and his mother, and flee to Egypt, and remain there till I tell you; for Herod is about to search for the child, to destroy him." And Joseph rose and took the child and his mother by night, and departed to Egypt, [15]and remained there until the death of Herod. This was to fulfill what the Lord had spoken by the prophet, "Out of Egypt have I called my son."

[19]But when Herod died, behold, an angel of the Lord appeared in a dream to Joseph in Egypt, saying, "Rise, take the child and his mother, and go to the land of Israel, for those who sought the child's life are dead." And Joseph rose and took the child and his mother, and went to the land of Israel. But when he heard that Archelaus reigned over Judea in place of his father Herod, he was afraid to go there, and being warned in a dream he withdrew to the district of Galilee. [23]And he went and dwelt in a city called Nazareth, that what was spoken by the prophets might be fulfilled, "He shall be called a Nazarene."

R E L THE EPIPHANY OF OUR LORD

FIRST READING

R L Isaiah 60:1–6
E Isaiah 60:1–6, 9

¹Arise, shine; for your light has come,
  and the glory of the LORD has risen upon you.
For behold, darkness shall cover the earth,
  and thick darkness the peoples;
but the LORD will arise upon you,
  and the glory of the LORD will be seen upon you.
And nations shall come to your light,
  and rulers to the brightness of your rising.
Lift up your eyes round about, and see;
  they all gather together, they come to you;
your sons shall come from far,
  and your daughters shall be carried in the arms.
Then you shall see and be radiant,
  your heart shall thrill and rejoice;
because the abundance of the sea shall be turned to you,
  the wealth of the nations shall come to you.
⁶A multitude of camels shall cover you,
  the young camels of Midian and Ephah;
  all those from Sheba shall come.
They shall bring gold and frankincense,
  and shall proclaim the praise of the LORD.
⁹For the coastlands shall wait for me,
  the ships of Tarshish first,
to bring your children from far,
  their silver and gold with them,
for the name of the LORD your God,
  and for the Holy One of Israel,
  because your God has glorified you.

SECOND READING

R Ephesians 3:2–3a, 5–6
E Ephesians 3:1–12
L Ephesians 3:2–12

¹For this reason I, Paul, a prisoner for Christ Jesus on behalf of you Gentiles—²assuming that you have heard of the stewardship of God's grace that was given to me for you, ³ᵃhow the mystery was made known to me by revelation, ³ᵇas I have written briefly. When you read this you can perceive my insight into the mystery of Christ, ⁵which was not made known to people of other generations as it has now been revealed to his holy apostles and prophets by the Spirit; ⁶that is, how the Gentiles are heirs with us, members of the same body, and partakers of the promise in Christ Jesus through the gospel.

⁷Of this gospel I was made a minister according to the gift of God's grace which was given me by the working of God's power. To me, though I am the very least of all the saints, this grace was given, to preach to the Gentiles the unsearchable riches of Christ, and to make everyone see what is the plan of the mystery hidden for ages in God who created all things; that through the church the manifold wisdom of God might now be made known to the principalities and powers in the heavenly places. This was according to the eternal purpose which God has realized in Christ Jesus our Lord, ¹²through faith in whom we have boldness and confidence of access to God.

GOSPEL

R E L Matthew 2:1–12

¹Now when Jesus was born in Bethlehem of Judea in the days of Herod the king, behold, magi from the East came to Jerusalem, saying, "Where is he who has been born king of the Jews? For we have seen his star in the East, and have come to worship him." When Herod the king heard this, he was troubled, and all Jerusalem with him; and assembling all the chief priests and scribes of the people, he inquired of them where the Christ was to be born. They told him, "In Bethlehem of Judea; for so it is written by the prophet:

'And you, O Bethlehem, in the land of Judah,
are by no means least among the rulers of Judah;
for from you shall come a ruler
who will govern my people Israel.' "

Then Herod summoned the magi secretly and ascertained from
them what time the star appeared; and he sent them to Bethlehem, saying, "Go and search diligently for the child, and when
you have found him bring me word, that I too may come and
worship." When they had heard the king they went their way;
and lo, the star which they had seen in the East went before
them, till it came to rest over the place where the child was.
When they saw the star, they rejoiced exceedingly with great
joy; and going into the house they saw the child with Mary his
mother, and they fell down and worshiped him. Then, opening
their treasures, they offered him gifts, gold and frankincense,
and myrrh. [12]And being warned in a dream not to return to
Herod, they departed to their own country by another way.

R L BAPTISM OF OUR LORD
E FIRST SUNDAY AFTER THE EPIPHANY

FIRST READING

R   Isaiah 42:1–4, 6–7
E   Isaiah 42:1–9
L   Isaiah 42:1–7

¹Behold my servant, whom I uphold,
   my chosen, in whom my soul delights,
upon whom I have put my Spirit,
   to bring forth justice to the nations:
not crying out, not lifting up his voice,
   not making it heard in the street,
a bruised reed my servant will not break,
   nor quench a dimly burning wick,
   but will faithfully bring forth justice.
⁴My chosen one will not fail or be discouraged
   till he has established justice in the earth;
   and the coastlands wait for his law.
⁵Thus says God, the LORD,
   who created the heavens and stretched them out,
   who spread forth the earth and what comes from it,
who gives breath to the people upon it
   and spirit to those who walk in it:
⁶"I am the LORD, I have called you in righteousness,
   I have taken you by the hand and kept you;
I have given you as a covenant to the people,
   a light to the nations,
   ⁷to open the eyes that are blind,
to bring out the prisoners from the dungeon,
   from the prison those who sit in darkness.
⁸I am the LORD, that is my name;
   my glory I give to no other,
   nor my praise to graven images.
⁹Behold, the former things have come to pass,
   and new things I now declare;
before they spring forth
   I tell you of them."

SECOND READING

R E L   Acts 10:34-38

[34]Peter opened his mouth and said: "Truly I perceive that God shows no partiality, but in every nation any one who is God-fearing and does what is right is acceptable to God. You know the word which God sent to Israel, preaching good news of peace by Jesus Christ (who is Lord of all), the word which was proclaimed throughout all Judea, beginning from Galilee after the baptism which John preached: [38]how God anointed Jesus of Nazareth with the Holy Spirit and with power; how Jesus went about doing good and healing all that were oppressed by the devil, for God was with him."

GOSPEL

R E L   Matthew 3:13-17

[13]Then Jesus came from Galilee to the Jordan to John, to be baptized by him. John would have prevented Jesus, saying, "I need to be baptized by you, and do you come to me?" But Jesus answered John, "Let it be so now; for thus it is fitting for us to fulfill all righteousness." Then John consented. And when Jesus was baptized, he went up immediately from the water, and behold, the heavens were opened and Jesus saw the Spirit of God descending like a dove, and alighting on him; [17]and lo, a voice from heaven, saying, "This is my Son, the beloved one, with whom I am well pleased."

FIRST READING

R   Isaiah 49:3, 5–6
E   Isaiah 49:1–7
L   Isaiah 49:1–6

> ¹Listen to me, O coastlands,
>   and hearken, you peoples from afar.
> The LORD called me from the womb,
>   from the body of my mother named my name.
> The LORD made my mouth like a sharp sword;
>   I was hid in the shadow of God's hand;
> the LORD made me a polished arrow,
>   I was hid away in God's quiver.
> ³And the LORD said to me, "You are my servant,
>   Israel, in whom I will be glorified."
> ⁴But I said, "I have labored in vain,
>   I have spent my strength for nothing and vanity;
> yet surely my right is with the LORD,
>   and my recompense with my God."
> ⁵And now the LORD says,
>   who formed me as a servant from the womb,
> to bring Jacob back to God
>   and to gather Israel to the LORD,
> for I am honored in the eyes of the LORD,
>   and my God has become my strength—
> ⁶the LORD says:
> "It is too light a thing that you should be my servant
>   to raise up the tribes of Jacob
>   and to restore the preserved of Israel:
> I will give you as a light to the nations,
>   that my salvation may reach to the end of the earth."
> ⁷Thus says the LORD,
>   the Redeemer of Israel, the Holy One of Israel,
> to one deeply despised, abhorred by the nations,
>   the servant of rulers:

"Monarchs shall see and arise;
  chieftans, and they shall prostrate themselves;
because of the LORD, who is faithful,
  the Holy One of Israel, who has chosen you."

SECOND READING

R 1 Corinthians 1:1–3
E L 1 Corinthians 1:1–9

¹Paul, called by the will of God to be an apostle of Christ Jesus, and our brother Sosthenes,

To the church of God which is at Corinth, to those sanctified in Christ Jesus, called to be saints together with all those who in every place call on the name of our Lord Jesus Christ, both their Lord and ours:

³Grace to you and peace from God, our Father, and the Lord Jesus Christ.

⁴I give thanks to God always for you because of the grace of God which was given you in Christ Jesus, that in every way you were enriched in Christ with all speech and all knowledge—even as the testimony to Christ was confirmed among you—so that you are not lacking in any spiritual gift, as you wait for the revealing of our Lord Jesus Christ; who will sustain you to the end, guiltless in the day of our Lord Jesus Christ. ⁹God is faithful, by whom you were called into the communion of the Son of God, Jesus Christ our Lord.

GOSPEL

R John 1:29–34
E L John 1:29–41

²⁹The next day John saw Jesus coming toward him, and said, "Behold, the Lamb of God, who takes away the sin of the world! This is the one of whom I said, 'After me comes a man who ranks before me, for he was before me.' I myself did not know him; but for this I came baptizing with water, that he might be revealed to Israel." And John bore witness, "I saw the Spirit descend as a dove from heaven, and it remained on him.

I myself did not know him; but the one who sent me to baptize with water said to me, 'The one on whom you see the Spirit descend and remain, this is the one who baptizes with the Holy Spirit.' ³⁴And I have seen and have borne witness that this is the Son of God."

³⁵The next day again John was standing with two of his disciples; and seeing Jesus walking, he said, "Behold, the Lamb of God!" The two disciples heard him say this, and they followed Jesus. Jesus turned, and saw them following, and said to them, "What do you seek?" And they said to him, "Rabbi (which means Teacher), where are you staying?" Jesus said to them, "Come and see." They came and saw where Jesus was staying; and they stayed with him that day, for it was about the tenth hour. One of the two who heard John speak, and followed him, was Andrew, Simon Peter's brother. ⁴¹Andrew first found his brother Simon, and said to him, "We have found the Messiah" (which means Christ).

R THIRD SUNDAY IN ORDINARY TIME
E L THIRD SUNDAY AFTER THE EPIPHANY

FIRST READING

R Isaiah 8:23b–9:3
L Isaiah 9:1b–4

[23b/1b]In the former time God brought into contempt the land of Zebulun and the land of Naphtali, but in the latter time God will make glorious the way of the sea, the land beyond the Jordan, Galilee of the nations.

The people who walked in darkness
　　have seen a great light;
those who dwelt in a land of deep darkness,
　　on them has light shined.
[3]You have multiplied the nation,
　　you have increased its joy;
they rejoice before you
　　as with joy at the harvest,
　　as they rejoice when dividing spoil.
[4]For the yoke of their burden,
　　and the staff of their shoulders,
　　the rod of their oppressor,
　　you have broken as in the day of Midian.

E Amos 3:1–8

[1]Hear this word that the LORD has spoken against you, O people of Israel, against the whole family which I brought up out of the land of Egypt:
"You only have I known
　　of all families of the earth;
therefore I will punish you
　　for all your iniquities.
Do two walk together,
　　unless they have made an appointment?
Does the lion roar in the forest,
　　when it has no prey?

Does a young lion cry out from its den,
　　if it has taken nothing?
Does a bird fall in a snare on the earth,
　　when there is no trap for it?
Does a snare spring up from the ground,
　　when it has taken nothing?
Is a trumpet blown in a city,
　　and the people are not afraid?
Does evil befall a city,
　　unless the LORD has done it?
Surely the Lord GOD does nothing,
　　without revealing the divine secret
　　to the prophets, the servants of the LORD.
8The lion has roared;
　　who will not fear?
The Lord GOD has spoken;
　　who can but prophesy?"

SECOND READING

R　1 Corinthians 1:10–13, 17
E　L　1 Corinthians 1:10–17

10I appeal to you, my dear people, by the name of our Lord
Jesus Christ, that all of you agree and that there be no dissen-
sions among you, but that you be united in the same mind and
the same judgment. For it has been reported to me by Chloe's
people that there is quarreling among you, my dear people.
What I mean is that each one of you says, "I belong to Paul,"
or "I belong to Apollos," or "I belong to Cephas," or "I belong
to Christ." 13Is Christ divided? Was Paul crucified for you? Or
were you baptized in the name of Paul? 14I am thankful that I
baptized none of you except Crispus and Gaius; lest any one
should say that you were baptized in my name. (I did baptize
also the household of Stephanas. Beyond that, I do not know
whether I baptized any one else.) 17For Christ did not send me
to baptize but to preach the gospel, and not with eloquent wisdom, lest the cross of Christ be emptied of its power.

GOSPEL

R E L Matthew 4:12–23

[12]Now when Jesus heard that John had been arrested, he withdrew into Galilee; and leaving Nazareth he went and dwelt in Capernaum by the sea, in the territory of Zebulun and Naphtali, that what was spoken by the prophet Isaiah might be fulfilled:

"The land of Zebulun and the land of Naphtali,
toward the sea, across the Jordan,
Galilee of the Gentiles—
the people who sat in darkness
have seen a great light,
and for those who sat in the region and shadow of death
light has dawned."

From that time Jesus began to preach, saying, "Repent, for the dominion of heaven is at hand."

Walking by the Sea of Galilee, Jesus saw two brothers, Simon who is called Peter and Andrew his brother, casting a net into the sea; for they were fishermen. And Jesus said to them, "Follow me, and I will make you fish for human beings." Immediately they left their nets and followed Jesus. And going on from there Jesus saw two other brothers, James the son of Zebedee and John his brother, in the boat with Zebedee their father, mending their nets, and Jesus called them. Immediately they left the boat and their father, and followed Jesus.

[23]And Jesus went about all Galilee, teaching in their synagogues and preaching the gospel of the dominion of heaven and healing every disease and every infirmity among the people.

R FOURTH SUNDAY IN ORDINARY TIME
E L FOURTH SUNDAY AFTER THE EPIPHANY

FIRST READING

R Zephaniah 2:3, 3:12–13

³Seek the LORD, all you humble of the land,
    who do the commands of the LORD;
seek righteousness, seek humility;
    perhaps you may be hidden
    on the day of the wrath of the LORD.
¹²"For I will leave in the midst of you
    a people humble and lowly.
They will seek refuge in the name of the LORD,
    ¹³those who are left in Israel;
they shall do no wrong
    and utter no lies,
nor shall there be found in their mouth
    a deceitful tongue.
For they shall pasture and lie down,
    and none shall make them afraid."

E L Micah 6:1–8

¹Hear what the LORD says:
Arise, plead your case before the mountains,
    and let the hills hear your voice.
Hear, you mountains, the controversy of the LORD,
    and you enduring foundations of the earth;
for the LORD has a controversy with the people of God;
    the LORD will contend with Israel.
"O my people, what have I done to you?
    In what have I wearied you? Answer me!
For I brought you up from the land of Egypt,
    and redeemed you from the house of bondage;
and I sent before you Moses,
    Aaron, and Miriam.
O my people, remember what Balak king of Moab devised,
    and what Balaam the son of Beor answered him,

and what happened from Shittim to Gilgal,
   that you may know the saving acts of the LORD."
"With what shall I come before the LORD,
   and bow myself before God on high?
Shall I come before God with burnt offerings,
   with calves a year old?
Will the LORD be pleased with thousands of rams,
   with ten thousand rivers of oil?
Shall I give my first-born for my transgression,
   the fruit of my body for the sin of my soul?"
⁸The LORD has showed you, O human one, what is good;
   and what does the LORD require of you
but to do justice, and to love kindness,
   and to walk humbly with your God?

SECOND READING

R E L   1 Corinthians 1:26–31

²⁶For consider your call, my dear people; not many of you were
wise according to worldly standards, not many were powerful,
not many were of noble birth; but God chose what is foolish in
the world to shame the wise, God chose what is weak in the
world to shame the strong, God chose what is low and despised in the world, even things that are not, to bring to nothing things that are, so that no human being might boast in the
presence of God. God is the source of your life in Christ Jesus,
whom God made our wisdom, our righteousness and sanctification and redemption; ³¹therefore, as it is written, "Let those
who boast, boast of the Lord."

GOSPEL

R   Matthew 5:1–12a
E L   Matthew 5:1–12

¹Seeing the crowds, Jesus went up on the mountain and sat
down, and his disciples came to him. And Jesus opened his
mouth and taught them, saying:

"Blessed are the poor in spirit, for theirs is the dominion of
heaven.

"Blessed are those who mourn, for they shall be comforted.

"Blessed are the meek, for they shall inherit the earth.

"Blessed are those who hunger and thirst for righteousness, for they shall be satisfied.

"Blessed are the merciful, for they shall obtain mercy.

"Blessed are the pure in heart, for they shall see God.

"Blessed are the peacemakers, for they shall be called children of God.

"Blessed are those who are persecuted for righteousness' sake, for theirs is the dominion of heaven.

"Blessed are you when you are reviled and persecuted and all kinds of evil is uttered against you falsely on my account. [12a]Rejoice and be glad, for your reward is great in heaven, [12b]for the prophets who were before you were persecuted in the same way."

R FIFTH SUNDAY IN ORDINARY TIME
E L FIFTH SUNDAY AFTER THE EPIPHANY

FIRST READING

R Isaiah 58:7–10
L Isaiah 58:5–9a

5"Is such the fast that I choose,
  a day for people to humble themselves?
Is it to bow down their head like a rush,
  and to spread sackcloth and ashes under them?
Will you call this a fast,
  and a day acceptable to the LORD?
Is not this the fast that I choose:
    to loose the bonds of wickedness,
    to undo the thongs of the yoke,
  to let the oppressed go free,
    and to break every yoke?
7Is it not to share your bread with the hungry,
  and bring the homeless poor into your house;
when you see the naked, to cover them,
  and not to hide yourselves from your own flesh?
Then shall your light break forth like the dawn,
  and your healing shall spring up speedily;
your righteousness shall go before you,
  the glory of the LORD shall be your rear guard.
9aThen you shall call, and the LORD will answer;
  you shall cry, and God will say, Here I am.
9bIf you take away from the midst of you the yoke,
  the pointing of the finger, and speaking wickedness,
10if you pour yourselves out for the hungry
  and satisfy the desire of the afflicted,
then shall your light rise in the darkness
  and your gloom be as the noonday."

E Habakkuk 3:1–6, 17–19

1A prayer of Habakkuk the prophet, according to Shigionoth.
O LORD, I have heard the report of you,
  and your work, O LORD, do I fear.

In the midst of the years renew it;
　　in the midst of the years make it known;
　　in wrath remember mercy.
God came from Teman,
　　and the Holy One from Mount Paran.
God's glory covered the heavens,
　　the earth was full of the praise of the LORD,
whose brightness was like the light;
　　rays flashed from God's hand;
　　and there God's power was veiled.
Before God went pestilence,
　　and plague followed close behind.
⁶God stood and measured the earth,
　　looked and shook the nations;
then the eternal mountains were scattered,
　　the everlasting hills sank low.
　　God's ways were as of old.
¹⁷Though the fig tree does not blossom,
　　nor fruit be on the vines,
the produce of the olive fail
　　and the fields yield no food,
the flock be cut off from the fold
　　and there be no herd in the stalls,
yet I will rejoice in the LORD,
　　I will joy in the God of my salvation.
¹⁹GOD, the Lord, is my strength;
　　God makes my feet like hinds' feet,
　　making me tread upon my high places.

SECOND READING

R　L　1 Corinthians 2:1–5
　　E　1 Corinthians 2:1–11

¹When I came to you, my dear people, I did not come pro-
claiming to you the testimony of God in lofty words or wisdom. For I decided to know nothing among you except Jesus
Christ and him crucified. And I was with you in weakness and
in much fear and trembling; and my speech and my message
were not in plausible words of wisdom, but in demonstration

of the Spirit and of power, [5]that your faith might not rest in human wisdom but in the power of God.

[6]Yet among the mature we do impart wisdom, although it is not a wisdom of this age or of the rulers of this age, who are doomed to pass away. But we impart a secret and hidden wisdom of God, which God decreed before the ages for our glorification. None of the rulers of this age understood this; for if they had, they would not have crucified the Lord of glory. But, as it is written,

"What no eye has seen, nor ear heard,
nor human heart conceived,
what God has prepared for those who love God,"

God has revealed to us through the Spirit. For the Spirit searches everything, even the depths of God. [11]For what human being knows a person's thoughts except the very spirit of that person? So also no one comprehends the thoughts of God except the Spirit of God.

GOSPEL

R   Matthew 5:13–16
E L   Matthew 5:13–20

[At that time Jesus said,]

[13]"You are the salt of the earth; but if salt has lost its taste, how shall its saltness be restored? It is no longer good for anything except to be thrown out and trodden under foot.

"You are the light of the world. A city set on a hill cannot be hid. Nor do people light a lamp and put it under a bushel, but on a stand, and it gives light to all in the house. [16]Let your light so shine before others, that they may see your good works and give glory to your Father who is in heaven.

[17]"Think not that I have come to abolish the law and the prophets; I have come not to abolish them but to fulfill them. For truly, I say to you, till heaven and earth pass away, not an iota, not a dot, will pass from the law until all is accomplished. Whoever then relaxes one of the least of these commandments

and teaches people so, shall be called least in the dominion of heaven; but whoever does them and teaches them shall be called great in the dominion of heaven. [20]For I tell you, unless your righteousness exceeds that of the scribes and Pharisees, you will never enter the dominion of heaven."

R SIXTH SUNDAY IN ORDINARY TIME
E L SIXTH SUNDAY AFTER THE EPIPHANY
E PROPER 1

FIRST READING

R Sirach 15:15–20
E Sirach 15:11–20

> [11]Do not say, "Because of the Lord I left the right way";
>   for the Lord will not do what the Lord hates.
> Do not say, "It was the Lord who led me astray";
>   for the Lord has no need of a sinner.
> The Lord hates all abominations,
>   and abominations are not loved by the God-fearing.
> It was the Lord who created human beings in the beginning,
>   and left them in the power of their own inclination.
> [15]If you will, you can keep the commandments,
>   and to act faithfully is a matter of your own choice.
> The Lord has placed before you fire and water:
>   stretch out your hand for whichever you wish.
> Set before human beings are life and death,
>   and whichever they choose will be given to them.
> For great is the wisdom of the Lord;
>   the Lord is mighty in power and sees everything;
> the eyes of the Lord are on the God-fearing,
>   and the Lord knows every human deed.
> [20]The Lord has not commanded any one to be ungodly,
>   and has not given any one permission to sin.

L Deuteronomy 30:15–20

> [15]"See, I have set before you this day life and good, death and
> evil. If you obey the commandments of the LORD your God
> which I command you this day, by loving the LORD your God,
> by walking in the LORD's ways, and by keeping God's com-
> mandments and statutes and ordinances, then you shall live
> and multiply, and the LORD your God will bless you in the land
> which you are entering to take possession of it. But if your
> heart turns away, and you will not hear, but are drawn away
> to worship other gods and serve them, I declare to you this

day, that you shall perish; you shall not live long in the land which you are going over the Jordan to enter and possess. I call heaven and earth to witness against you this day, that I have set before you life and death, blessing and curse; therefore choose life, that you and your descendants may live, [20]loving the LORD your God, obeying the LORD's voice, and cleaving to God; for that means life to you and length of days, that you may dwell in the land which the LORD swore to your forebears, to Abraham, to Isaac, and to Jacob, to give them."

SECOND READING

R 1 Corinthians 2:6–10
L 1 Corinthians 2:6–13

[6]Among the mature we do impart wisdom, although it is not a wisdom of this age or of the rulers of this age, who are doomed to pass away. But we impart a secret and hidden wisdom of God, which God decreed before the ages for our glorification. None of the rulers of this age understood this; for if they had, they would not have crucified the Lord of glory. But, as it is written,

"What no eye has seen, nor ear heard,
nor human heart conceived,
what God has prepared for those who love God,"

[10]God has revealed to us through the Spirit. For the Spirit searches everything, even the depths of God. [11]For what human being knows a person's thoughts except the very spirit of that person? So also no one comprehends the thoughts of God except the Spirit of God. Now we have received not the spirit of the world, but the Spirit which is from God, that we might understand the gifts bestowed on us by God. [13]And we impart this in words not taught by human wisdom but taught by the Spirit, interpreting spiritual truths to those who possess the Spirit.

E 1 Corinthians 3:1–9

[1]My dear people, I could not address you as spiritual people, but as fleshly people, as infants in Christ. I fed you with milk, not solid food; for you were not ready for it; and even yet you

are not ready, for you are still of the flesh. For while there is jealousy and strife among you, are you not of the flesh, and behaving like ordinary human beings? For when one says, "I belong to Paul," and another, "I belong to Apollos," are you not mere humans?

What then is Apollos? What is Paul? Servants through whom you believed, as the Lord assigned to each. I planted, Apollos watered, but God gave the growth. So neither the one who plants nor the one who waters is anything, but only God who gives the growth. The one who plants and the one who waters are equal, and all shall receive their wages according to their labor. ⁹For we are God's co-workers; you are God's field, God's building.

GOSPEL

R   Matthew 5:17–37
E   Matthew 5:21–24, 27–30, 33–37
L   Matthew 5:20–37

[At that time Jesus said,]

¹⁷"Think not that I have come to abolish the law and the prophets; I have come not to abolish them but to fulfill them. For truly, I say to you, till heaven and earth pass away, not an iota, not a dot, will pass from the law until all is accomplished. Whoever then relaxes one of the least of these commandments and teaches people so, shall be called least in the dominion of heaven; but whoever does them and teaches them shall be called great in the dominion of heaven. ²⁰For I tell you, unless your righteousness exceeds that of the scribes and Pharisees, you will never enter the dominion of heaven.

²¹"You have heard that it was said to those of old, 'You shall not kill; and whoever kills shall be liable to judgment.' But I say to you that everyone who is angry with a brother or sister shall be liable to judgment; whoever insults a brother or sister shall be liable to the council, and whoever says, 'You fool!' shall be liable to the hell of fire. So if you are offering your gift at the altar, and there remember that your brother or sister has something against you, ²⁴leave your gift there before the altar

and go; first be reconciled to your brother or sister, and then come and offer your gift. ²⁵Make friends quickly with your accuser, while you are going together to court, lest your accuser hand you over to the judge, and the judge to the guard, and you be put in prison; truly, I say to you, you will never get out till you have paid the last penny.

²⁷"You have heard that it was said, 'You shall not commit adultery.' But I say to you that every man who looks at a woman lustfully has already committed adultery with her in his heart. If your right eye causes you to sin, pluck it out and throw it away; it is better that you lose one part of your body than that your whole body be thrown into hell. ³⁰And if your right hand causes you to sin, cut it off and throw it away; it is better that you lose one part of your body than that your whole body go into hell.

³¹"It was also said, 'Whatever man divorces his wife, let him give her a certificate of divorce.' But I say to you that every man who divorces his wife, except on the ground of unchastity, makes her an adulteress; and whatever man marries a divorced woman commits adultery.

³³"Again you have heard that it was said to those of old, 'You shall not swear falsely, but shall perform to the Lord what you have sworn.' But I say to you, Do not swear at all, either by heaven, for it is the throne of God, or by the earth, for it is God's footstool, or by Jerusalem, for it is the city of the great Sovereign. And do not swear by your head, for you cannot make one hair white or black. ³⁷Let what you say be simply 'Yes' or 'No'; anything more than this comes from evil."

R SEVENTH SUNDAY IN ORDINARY TIME
E L SEVENTH SUNDAY AFTER THE EPIPHANY
E PROPER 2

FIRST READING

R L Leviticus 19:1–2, 17–18
  E Leviticus 19:1–2, 9–18

¹The LORD said to Moses, ²"Say to all the congregation of the people of Israel, You shall be holy; for I the LORD your God am holy.

⁹"When you reap the harvest of your land, you shall not reap your field to its very border, neither shall you gather the gleanings after your harvest. And you shall not strip your vineyard bare, neither shall you gather the fallen grapes of your vineyard; you shall leave them for the poor and for the sojourner: I am the LORD your God.

"You shall not steal, nor deal falsely, nor lie to one another. And you shall not swear by my name falsely, and so profane the name of your God: I am the LORD.

"You shall not oppress or rob your neighbor. The wages of a hired servant shall not remain with you all night until the morning. You shall not curse the deaf or put a stumbling block before the blind, but you shall fear your God: I am the LORD.

"You shall do no injustice in judgment; you shall not be partial to the poor or defer to the great, but in righteousness shall you judge your neighbor. You shall not go up and down as a slanderer among your people, and you shall not stand forth against the life of your neighbor: I am the LORD.

¹⁷"You shall not hate your neighbor in your heart, but you shall reason with your neighbor, lest you thereby bear sin. ¹⁸You shall not take vengeance or bear any grudge against your own people, but you shall love your neighbor as yourself: I am the LORD."

SECOND READING

R 1 Corinthians 3:16–23
E L 1 Corinthians 3:10–11, 16–23

[10]According to the grace of God given to me, like a wise expert builder I laid a foundation, and another is building upon it. Let all take care how they build upon it. [11]For no other foundation can any one lay than that which is laid, which is Jesus Christ.

[16]Do you not know that you are God's temple and that God's Spirit dwells in you? Any one destroying God's temple will be destroyed by God. For God's temple is holy, and that temple you are.

Do not deceive yourselves. If any among you thinks that you are wise in this age, then become a fool that you may become wise. For the wisdom of this world is folly with God. For it is written, "God catches the wise in their craftiness," and again, "The Lord knows that the thoughts of the wise are futile." So let no one make a human boast. For all things are yours, whether Paul or Apollos or Cephas or the world or life or death or the present or the future, all are yours; [23]and you are Christ's; and Christ is God's.

GOSPEL

R E L Matthew 5:38–48

[At that time Jesus said,]

[38]"You have heard that it was said, 'An eye for an eye and a tooth for a tooth.' But I say to you, Do not resist one who is evil. But if any one strikes you on the right cheek, offer the other also; and if any one would sue you and take your coat, give up your cloak as well; and if any one forces you to go one mile, go along together for two miles. Give to whoever begs from you, and do not refuse any who would borrow from you.

"You have heard that it was said, 'You shall love your neighbor and hate your enemy.' But I say to you, Love your enemies and pray for those who persecute you, so that you may be children of your Father who is in heaven; for God makes the sun to rise on the evil and on the good, and sends rain on the just and on the unjust. For if you love those who love you, what reward have you? Do not even the tax collectors do the same? And if you salute only your own, what more are you doing than others? Do not even the Gentiles do the same? [48]You, therefore, must be perfect, as your heavenly Father is perfect."

R EIGHTH SUNDAY IN ORDINARY TIME
E L EIGHTH SUNDAY AFTER THE EPIPHANY
E PROPER 3

FIRST READING

R   Isaiah 49:14–15
E   Isaiah 49:8–18
L   Isaiah 49:13–18

⁸Thus says the LORD;
"In a time of favor I have answered you,
    in a day of salvation I have helped you;
I have kept you and given you
    as a covenant to the people,
to establish the land,
    to apportion the desolate heritages;
saying to the prisoners, 'Come forth,'
    to those who are in darkness, 'Appear.'
They shall feed along the ways,
    on all bare heights shall be their pasture;
they shall not hunger or thirst,
    neither scorching wind nor sun shall smite them,
for the one who has pity on them will lead them,
    and by springs of water will guide them.
And I will make all my mountains a way,
    and my highways shall be raised up.
Lo, these shall come from afar,
    and lo, these from the north and from the west,
    and these from the land of Syene."
¹³Sing for joy, O heavens, and exult, O earth;
    break forth, O mountains, into singing!
For the LORD has comforted the people,
    and will have compassion on God's afflicted.
¹⁴But Zion said, "The LORD has forsaken me,
    my Lord has forgotten me."
¹⁵"Can a woman forget her nursing infant
    that she should have no compassion on the child of her
    womb?

Even these may forget,
   yet I will not forget you.
¹⁶Behold, I have graven you on the palms of my hands;
   your walls are continually before me.
Your builders outstrip your destroyers,
   and those who laid you waste go forth from you.
¹⁸Lift up your eyes round about and see;
   they all gather, they come to you.
As I live, says the Lord,
   you shall put them all on as an ornament,
   you shall bind them on as a bride does."

SECOND READING

R   1 Corinthians 4:1–5
E   1 Corinthians 4:1–5, 8–13
L   1 Corinthians 4:1–13

¹This is how one should regard us, as servants of Christ and stewards of the mysteries of God. Moreover it is required of stewards that they be found trustworthy. But with me it is a very small thing that I should be judged by you or by any human court. I do not even judge myself. I am not aware of anything against myself, but I am not thereby acquitted. It is the Lord who judges me. ⁵Therefore do not pronounce judgment before the time, before the Lord comes, who will bring to light the things now hidden in darkness and will disclose the purposes of the heart. Then everyone's commendation will come from God.

⁶I have applied all this to myself and Apollos for your benefit, my dear people, that you may learn by us not to go beyond what is written, that none of you may be puffed up in favor of one against another. For who sees anything different in you? What have you that you did not receive? If then you received it, why do you boast as if it were not a gift?

⁸Already you are filled! Already you have become rich! Without us you have become reigning monarchs! And would that you did reign, so that we might share the rule with you! For I think that God has exhibited us apostles as last of all, like those sen-

tenced to death; because we have become a spectacle to the world, to angels and to humanity. We are fools for Christ's sake, but you are wise in Christ. We are weak, but you are strong. You are held in honor, but we in disrepute. To the present hour we hunger and thirst, we are ill-clad and buffeted and homeless, and we labor, working with our own hands. When reviled, we bless; when persecuted, we endure; [13]when slandered, we try to conciliate; we have become, and are now, as the refuse of the world, the offscouring of all things.

GOSPEL

R E L Matthew 6:24–34

[At that time Jesus said,]

[24]"No one can be slave to two masters; for either you will hate the one and love the other, or you will be devoted to the one and despise the other. You cannot serve God and mammon.

"Therefore I tell you, do not be anxious about your life, what you shall eat or what you shall drink, nor about your body, what you shall put on. Is not life more than food, and the body more than clothing? Look at the birds of the air: they neither sow nor reap nor gather into barns, and yet your heavenly Father feeds them. Are you not of more value than they? And which of you by being anxious can add one cubit to your span of life? And why are you anxious about clothing? Consider the lilies of the field, how they grow; they neither toil nor spin; yet I tell you, even Solomon in all his glory was not arrayed like one of these. But if God so clothes the grass of the field, which today is alive and tomorrow is thrown into the oven, will God not much more clothe you, O you of little faith? Therefore do not be anxious, saying, 'What shall we eat?' or 'What shall we drink?' or 'What shall we wear?' For the Gentiles seek all these things; and your heavenly Father knows that you need them all. But seek first the dominion and the righteousness of God, and all these things shall be yours as well.

[34]"Therefore do not be anxious about tomorrow, for tomorrow will be anxious for itself. Let the day's own trouble be sufficient for the day."

E LAST SUNDAY AFTER THE EPIPHANY
L TRANSFIGURATION OF OUR LORD

FIRST READING

E L Exodus 24:12, 15–18

¹²The LORD said to Moses, "Come up to me on the mountain, and wait there; and I will give you the tables of stone, with the law and the commandment, which I have written for their instruction."

¹⁵Then Moses went up on the mountain, and the cloud covered the mountain. The glory of the LORD settled on Mount Sinai, and the cloud covered it six days; and on the seventh day God called to Moses out of the midst of the cloud. Now the appearance of the glory of the LORD was like a devouring fire on the top of the mountain in the sight of the people of Israel. ¹⁸And Moses entered the cloud, and went up on the mountain. And Moses was on the mountain forty days and forty nights.

SECOND READING

E Philippians 3:7–14

⁷Whatever gain I had, I counted as loss for the sake of Christ. Indeed I count everything as loss because of the surpassing worth of knowing Christ Jesus my Lord, for whose sake I have suffered the loss of all things, and count them as refuse, in order that I may gain Christ and be found in him, not having a righteousness of my own, based on law, but that which is through faith in Christ, the righteousness from God that depends on faith; that I may know Christ and the power of his resurrection, and may share his sufferings, becoming like Christ in his death, that if possible I may attain the resurrection from the dead.

Not that I have already obtained this or am already perfect; but I press on to make it my own, because Christ Jesus has made me his own. My dear people, I do not consider that I have made it my own; but one thing I do, forgetting what lies behind and straining forward to what lies ahead, ¹⁴I press on toward the goal for the prize of the upward call of God in Christ Jesus.

L   2 Peter 1:16–19

¹⁶For we did not follow cleverly devised myths when we made known to you the power and coming of our Lord Jesus Christ, but we were eyewitnesses of his majesty. For when Jesus our Lord received honor and glory from God, the Father, and the voice was borne to him by the Majestic Glory, "This is my Son, my beloved one, with whom I am well pleased," we heard this voice borne from heaven, for we were with Jesus on the holy mountain. ¹⁹And we have the prophetic word made more sure. You will do well to pay attention to this as to a lamp shining in a dark place, until the day dawns and the morning star rises in your hearts.

GOSPEL

E L   Matthew 17:1–9

¹After six days Jesus took along Peter and James and John his brother, and led them up a high mountain apart. And Jesus was transfigured before them, and his face shone like the sun, and his garments became white as light. And behold, there appeared to them Moses and Elijah, talking with Jesus. And Peter said to Jesus, "Lord, it is well that we are here; if you wish, I will make three booths here, one for you and one for Moses and one for Elijah." Peter was still speaking, when lo, a bright cloud overshadowed them, and a voice from the cloud said, "This is my Son, the beloved one, with whom I am well pleased; listen to him." When the disciples heard this, they fell on their faces, and were filled with awe. But Jesus came and touched them, saying, "Rise, and have no fear." And when they lifted up their eyes, they saw no one but Jesus only.

⁹And as they were coming down the mountain, Jesus commanded them, "Tell no one the vision, until the Man of Heaven is raised from the dead."

FIRST READING

R   Joel 2:12–18
E   Joel 2:1–2, 12–17
L   Joel 2:12–19

[1]Blow the trumpet in Zion;
    sound the alarm on my holy mountain!
Let all the inhabitants of the land tremble,
    for the day of the LORD is coming, it is near,
[2]a day of darkness and gloom,
    a day of clouds and thick darkness!
Like blackness there is spread upon the mountains
    a great and powerful people;
their like has never been from of old,
    nor will be again after them
    through the years of all generations.
[12]"Yet even now," says the LORD,
    "return to me with all your heart,
with fasting, with weeping, and with mourning;
    and rend your hearts and not your garments."
Return to the LORD, your God,
    for the LORD is gracious and merciful,
slow to anger, and abounding in steadfast love,
    and repents of evil.
Who knows whether the LORD will not turn and repent,
    and leave behind a blessing,
a cereal offering and a drink offering
    for the LORD, your God?
Blow the trumpet in Zion;
    sanctify a fast;
call a solemn assembly;
    gather the people.
Sanctify the congregation;
    assemble the elders;
gather the children,
    even nursing infants.

Let the bridegroom leave his room,
　　and the bride her chamber.
¹⁷Between the vestibule and the altar
　　let the priests, the ministers of the LORD, weep
and say, "Spare your people, O LORD,
　　and make not your heritage a reproach,
　　a byword among the nations.
Why should they say among the peoples,
　　'Where is their God?' "
¹⁸Then the LORD became jealous for the holy land,
　　and had pity on the people of God.
¹⁹The LORD answered and said to this people,
"Behold, I am sending to you
　　grain, wine, and oil,
　　and you will be satisfied;
and I will no more make you
　　a reproach among the nations."

SECOND READING

R　2 Corinthians 5:20–6:2
E　2 Corinthians 5:20b–6:10
L　2 Corinthians 5:20b–6:2

²⁰ᵃWe are ambassadors for Christ, God appealing through us. ²⁰ᵇWe beseech you on behalf of Christ, be reconciled to God. For our sake God made the one who knew no sin to be sin, so that in Christ we might become the righteousness of God.

Working together with God, then, we entreat you not to accept God's grace in vain. ²For God says,

"At the acceptable time I have listened to you,
and helped you on the day of salvation."

Behold, now is the acceptable time; behold, now is the day of salvation. ³We put no obstacle in any one's way, so that no fault may be found with our ministry, but as servants of God we commend ourselves in every way: through great endurance, in afflictions, hardships, calamities, beatings, imprisonments, tumults, labors, watching, hunger; by purity, knowledge, forbearance, kindness, the Holy Spirit, genuine love, truthful speech, and the power of God; with the weapons of righteousness for the right hand and for the left; in honor and dishonor, in ill repute and good repute. We are treated as impostors, and yet are true; as unknown, and yet well known; as dying, and behold we live; as punished, and yet not killed; ^{10}as sorrowful, yet always rejoicing; as poor, yet making many rich; as having nothing, and yet possessing everything.

GOSPEL

R   Matthew 6:1–6, 16–18
E L   Matthew 6:1–6, 16–21

[At that time Jesus said,]

^{1}"Beware of practicing your piety before others in order to be seen by them; for then you will have no reward from your Father who is in heaven.

"Thus, when you give alms, sound no trumpet before you, as the hypocrites do in the synagogues and in the streets, that they may be praised by others. Truly, I say to you, they have received their reward. But when you give alms, do not let your left hand know what your right hand is doing, so that your alms may be in secret; and your Father who sees in secret will reward you.

"And when you pray, you must not be like the hypocrites; for they love to stand and pray in the synagogues and at the street corners, that they may be seen by others. Truly, I say to you, they have received their reward. ^{6}But when you pray, go into your room and shut the door and pray to your Father who is in secret; and your Father who sees in secret will reward you.

^{16}"And when you fast, do not look dismal, like the hypocrites, for they disfigure their faces that their fasting may be seen by others. Truly, I say to you, they have received their reward. But when you fast, anoint your head and wash your face, ^{18}that your fasting may not be seen by others but by your Father who is in secret; and your Father who sees in secret will reward you.

[19]"Do not lay up for yourselves treasures on earth, where moth and rust consume and where thieves break in and steal, but lay up for yourselves treasures in heaven, where neither moth nor rust consumes and where thieves do not break in and steal. [21]For where your treasure is, there will your heart be also."

FIRST READING

R Genesis 2:7–9, 3:1–7
E Genesis 2:4b–9, 15–17, 25–3:7
L Genesis 2:7–9, 15–17, 3:1–7

⁴ᵇIn the day that the LORD God made the earth and the heavens, when no plant of the field was yet in the earth and no herb of the field had yet sprung up—for the LORD God had not caused it to rain upon the earth, and there was no one to till the ground; but a mist went up from the earth and watered the whole face of the ground—then the LORD God formed a man of dust from the ground, and breathed into his nostrils the breath of life; and the man became a living being. And the LORD God planted a garden in Eden, in the east, and there the LORD God put the man who had been made. ⁹And out of the ground the LORD God made to grow every tree that is pleasant to the sight and good for food, the tree of life also in the midst of the garden, and the tree of the knowledge of good and evil.

¹⁵The LORD God took the man and put him in the garden of Eden to till it and keep it. And the LORD God commanded the man, saying, "You may freely eat of every tree of the garden; ¹⁷but of the tree of the knowledge of good and evil you shall not eat, for in the day that you eat of it you shall die."

²⁵And they both, the man and his wife, were naked, and were not ashamed.

¹Now the serpent was more subtle than any other wild creature that the LORD God had made. The serpent said to the woman, "Did God say, 'You shall not eat of any tree of the garden'?" And the woman said to the serpent, "We may eat of the fruit of the trees of the garden; but God said, 'You shall not eat of the fruit of the tree which is in the midst of the garden, neither shall you touch it, lest you die.'" But the serpent said to the woman, "You will not die. For God knows that when you eat of it your eyes will be opened, and you will be like God, knowing good and evil." So when the woman saw that the tree was good for food, and that it was a delight to the eyes, and that

the tree was to be desired to make one wise, she took of its fruit and ate; and she also gave some to her husband, and he ate. [7]Then the eyes of both were opened, and they knew that they were naked; and they sewed fig leaves together and made themselves aprons.

SECOND READING

R E   Romans 5:12–19
L   Romans 5:12, 17–19

[12]Therefore as sin came into the world through one human being and death through sin, and so death spread to all human beings because all humans sinned—[13]sin indeed was in the world before the law was given, but sin is not counted where there is no law. Yet death reigned from Adam to Moses, even over those whose sins were not like the transgression of Adam, who was a type of the one who was to come.

But the free gift is not like the trespass. For if many died through the trespass of one, much more have the grace of God and the free gift in the grace of that one person Jesus Christ abounded for many. And the free gift is not like the effect of that one person's sin. For the judgment following one trespass brought condemnation, but the free gift following many trespasses brings justification. [17]If, because of the trespass of one, death reigned through that one, much more will those who receive the abundance of grace and the free gift of righteousness reign in life through the one Jesus Christ.

Then as the trespass of one led to condemnation for all, so the act of righteousness of one leads to acquittal and life for all. [19]For as by the disobedience of one person many were made sinners, so by the obedience of one person many will be made righteous.

GOSPEL

R E L   Matthew 4:1–11

[1]Then Jesus was led up by the Spirit into the wilderness to be tempted by the devil. And Jesus fasted forty days and forty nights, and afterward he was hungry. And the tempter came

and said to him, "If you are the Son of God, command these stones to become loaves of bread." But Jesus answered, "It is written,

'Not by bread alone shall one live,
but by every word that proceeds from the mouth of God.'"

Then the devil took Jesus to the holy city, and set him on the pinnacle of the temple, and said to him, "If you are the Son of God, throw yourself down; for it is written,

'God will give you into the angels' charge,'

and

'On their hands they will bear you up,
lest you strike your foot against a stone.'"

Jesus said to the devil, "Again it is written, 'You shall not tempt the Lord your God.'" Again, the devil took Jesus to a very high mountain, and showed him all the dominions of the world and the glory of them; and the devil said to Jesus, "All these I will give you, if you will fall down and worship me." Then Jesus said to the devil, "Begone, Satan! for it is written,

'You shall worship the Lord your God;
the Lord alone shall you serve.'"

¹¹Then the devil left him, and behold, angels came and ministered to him.

FIRST READING

R   Genesis 12:1–4a
E L Genesis 12:1–8

¹Now the LORD said to Abram, "Go from your country and your kindred and your father's house to the land that I will show you. And I will make of you a great nation, and I will bless you, and make your name great, so that you will be a blessing. I will bless those who bless you, and those who curse you I will curse; and by you all the families of the earth shall bless themselves."

⁴ᵃSo Abram went, as the LORD had told him; and Lot went with him. ⁴ᵇAbram was seventy-five years old when he departed from Haran. And Abram took Sarai his wife, and Lot his brother's son, and all their possessions which they had gathered, and the persons that they had gotten in Haran; and they set forth to go to the land of Canaan. When they had come to the land of Canaan, Abram passed through the land to the place at Shechem, to the oak of Moreh. At that time the Canaanites were in the land. Then the LORD appeared to Abram, and said, "To your descendants I will give this land." So Abram built there an altar to the LORD, who had appeared to him. ⁸Thence he removed to the mountain on the east of Bethel, and pitched his tent, with Bethel on the west and Ai on the east; and there Abram built an altar to the LORD and called on the name of the LORD.

SECOND READING

R   2 Timothy 1:8b–10

⁸ᵇShare in suffering for the gospel in the power of God, who saved us and called us with a holy calling, not in virtue of our works but in virtue of God's own purpose and the grace which God gave us in Christ Jesus ages ago, ¹⁰and now has manifested through the appearing of our Savior Christ Jesus, who abolished death and brought life and immortality to light through the gospel.

E L   Romans 4:1–5, 13–17

¹What then shall we say about Abraham, our forebear according to the flesh? For if Abraham was justified by works, he has something to boast about, but not before God. For what does the scripture say? "Abraham believed God, and it was reckoned to him as righteousness." Now to those who work, their wages are not reckoned as a gift but as their due. ⁵And to those who do not work but trust the one who justifies the ungodly, their faith is reckoned as righteousness.

¹³The promise to Abraham and his descendants, that they should inherit the world, did not come through the law but through the righteousness of faith. If it is the adherents of the law who are to be the heirs, faith is null and the promise is void. For the law brings wrath, but where there is no law there is no transgression.

That is why it depends on faith, in order that the promise may rest on grace and be guaranteed to all Abraham's descendants—not only to the adherents of the law but also to those who share the faith of Abraham, for he is the father of us all, ¹⁷as it is written, "I have made you the father of many nations"—in the presence of the God in whom Abraham believed, who gives life to the dead and calls into existence the things that do not exist.

GOSPEL

R   Matthew 17:1–9

¹After six days Jesus took along Peter and James and John his brother, and led them up a high mountain apart. And Jesus was transfigured before them, and his face shone like the sun, and his garments became white as light. And behold, there appeared to them Moses and Elijah, talking with Jesus. And Peter said to Jesus, "Lord, it is well that we are here; if you wish, I will make three booths here, one for you and one for Moses and one for Elijah." Peter was still speaking, when lo, a bright cloud overshadowed them, and a voice from the cloud said, "This is my Son, the beloved one, with whom I am well

pleased; listen to him." When the disciples heard this, they fell on their faces, and were filled with awe. But Jesus came and touched them, saying, "Rise, and have no fear." And when they lifted up their eyes, they saw no one but Jesus only.

9And as they were coming down the mountain, Jesus commanded them, "Tell no one the vision, until the Man of Heaven is raised from the dead."

E   John 3:1–17

1Now there was one of the Pharisees, named Nicodemus, a ruler of the Jewish people. He came to Jesus by night and said to him, "Rabbi, we know that you are a teacher come from God; for no one can do these signs that you do, except with the presence of God." Jesus said to Nicodemus, "Truly, truly, I say to you, unless one is born anew, one cannot see the dominion of God." Nicodemus said to Jesus, "How can a person be born when that person is old? Can one enter a second time into the womb and be born?" Jesus answered, "Truly, truly, I say to you, unless one is born of water and the Spirit, one cannot enter the dominion of God. That which is born of the flesh is flesh, and that which is born of the Spirit is spirit. Do not marvel that I said to you, 'You must be born anew.' The wind blows where it wills, and you hear the sound of it, but you do not know whence it comes or whither it goes; so it is with every one who is born of the Spirit." Nicodemus said to Jesus, "How can this be?" Jesus answered him, "Are you a teacher of Israel, and yet you do not understand this? Truly, truly, I say to you, we speak of what we know, and bear witness to what we have seen; but you do not receive our testimony. If I have told you earthly things and you do not believe, how can you believe if I tell you heavenly things? No one has ascended into heaven but the one who descended from heaven, the Man of Heaven. And as Moses lifted up the serpent in the wilderness, so must the Man of Heaven be lifted up, that whoever believes in that one may have eternal life."

For God loved the world in this way, that God gave the Son, the only begotten one, that whoever believes in him should not perish but have eternal life. [17]For God sent the Son into the world, not to condemn the world, but that through the Son the world might be saved.

L   John 4:5–26

[5]Jesus came to a city of Samaria, called Sychar, near the field that Jacob gave to his son Joseph. Jacob's well was there, and so Jesus, wearied from the journey, sat down beside the well. It was about the sixth hour.

There came a woman of Samaria to draw water. Jesus said to her, "Give me a drink." For his disciples had gone away into the city to buy food. The Samaritan woman said to Jesus, "How is it that you, a Jewish man, ask a drink of me, a woman of Samaria?" For Judeans have no dealings with Samaritans. Jesus answered the woman, "If you knew the gift of God, and who it is that is saying to you, 'Give me a drink,' you would have asked him, and he would have given you living water." The woman said to him, "Sir, you have nothing to draw with, and the well is deep; where do you get that living water? Are you greater than our father Jacob, who gave us the well, and drank from it himself, and his children, and his cattle?" Jesus said to her, "Every one who drinks of this water will thirst again, but those who drink of the water that I shall give them will never thirst; the water that I shall give them will become in them a spring of water welling up to eternal life." The woman said to Jesus, "Sir, give me this water, that I may not thirst, nor come here to draw."

Jesus said to her, "Go, call your husband, and come here." The woman answered him, "I have no husband." Jesus said to her, "You are right in saying, 'I have no husband'; for you have had five husbands, and he whom you now have is not your husband; this you said truly." The woman said to Jesus, "Sir, I perceive that you are a prophet. Our forebears worshiped on this mountain; and you say that in Jerusalem is the place where it is proper to worship." Jesus said to her, "Woman, believe me, the hour is coming when neither on this mountain nor in Jerusalem will you worship the Father. You worship what you do not know; we worship what we know, for salvation is from the Jews. But the hour is coming, and now is, when the true worshipers will worship the Father in spirit and truth, for such worshipers the Father seeks. God is spirit, and those who worship God must worship in spirit and truth." The woman said to Jesus, "I know that Messiah is coming (the one who is called Christ); when that one comes, he will show us all things." [26]Jesus said to her, "I who speak to you am the one."

FIRST READING

R   Exodus 17:3–7
E   Exodus 17:1–7

¹All the congregation of the people of Israel moved on from the wilderness of Sin by stages, according to the commandment of the LORD, and camped at Rephidim; but there was no water for the people to drink. Therefore the people found fault with Moses, and said, "Give us water to drink." And Moses said to them, "Why do you find fault with me? Why do you put the LORD to the proof?" ³But the people thirsted there for water, and the people murmured against Moses, and said, "Why did you bring us up out of Egypt, to kill us and our children and our cattle with thirst?" So Moses cried to the LORD, "What shall I do with this people? They are almost ready to stone me." And the LORD said to Moses, "Pass on before the people, taking with you some of the elders of Israel; and take in your hand the rod with which you struck the Nile, and go. Behold, I will stand before you there on the rock at Horeb; and you shall strike the rock, and water shall come out of it, that the people may drink." And Moses did so, in the sight of the elders of Israel. ⁷And Moses called the name of the place Massah and Meribah, because of the faultfinding of the children of Israel, and because they put the LORD to the proof by saying, "Is the LORD among us or not?"

L   Isaiah 42:14–21

¹⁴For a long time I have held my peace,
   I have kept still and restrained myself;
now I will cry out like a woman in labor,
   I will gasp and pant.
I will lay waste mountains and hills,
   and dry up all their herbage;
I will turn the rivers into islands,
   and dry up the pools.
And I will lead the blind
   in a way that they know not,

in paths that they have not known
   I will guide them.
I will turn the darkness before them into light,
   the rough places into level ground.
These are the things I will do,
   and I will not forsake them.
They shall be turned back and utterly put to shame,
   who trust in graven images,
who say to molten images,
   "You are our gods."
Hear, you deaf;
   and look, you blind, that you may see!
Who is blind but my servant,
   or deaf as my messenger whom I send?
Who is blind as my dedicated one,
   or blind as the servant of the LORD?
My servant sees many things, but does not observe them;
   with open ears, my servant does not hear.
²¹Out of divine righteousness the LORD was pleased
   to magnify the law and make it glorious.

SECOND READING

R   Romans 5:1–2, 5–8
E   Romans 5:1–11

¹Therefore, since we are justified by faith, we have peace with God through our Lord Jesus Christ, ²through whom we have obtained access to this grace in which we stand, and we rejoice in our hope of sharing the glory of God. ³More than that, we rejoice in our sufferings, knowing that suffering produces endurance, and endurance produces character, and character produces hope, ⁵and hope does not disappoint us, because God's love has been poured into our hearts through the Holy Spirit which has been given to us.

While we were still weak, at the right time Christ died for the ungodly. Why, one will hardly die for a righteous person—though perhaps for a good person one will dare even to die. ⁸But God's own love is shown for us in what while we were yet sinners Christ died for us. ⁹Since, therefore, we are now justified by the blood of Christ, much more shall we be saved by him from the wrath of God. For if while we were enemies we were reconciled to God by the death of the Son of God, much more, now that we are reconciled, shall we be saved by the life of the Son of God. ¹¹Not only so, but we also rejoice in God through our Lord Jesus Christ, through whom we have now received our reconciliation.

L   Ephesians 5:8–14

⁸Once you were darkness, but now you are light in the Lord; walk as children of light (for the fruit of light is found in all that is good and right and true), and try to learn what is pleasing to the Lord. Take no part in the unfruitful works of darkness, but instead expose them. For it is a shame even to speak of the things that they do in secret; but when anything is exposed by the light it becomes visible, for anything that becomes visible is light. ¹⁴Therefore it is said,

"Awake, O sleeper, and arise from the dead,
and Christ shall give you light."

GOSPEL

R   John 4:5–42
E   John 4:5–26, 39–42

⁵Jesus came to a city of Samaria, called Sychar, near the field that Jacob gave to his son Joseph. Jacob's well was there, and so Jesus, wearied from the journey, sat down beside the well. It was about the sixth hour.

There came a woman of Samaria to draw water. Jesus said to her, "Give me a drink." For his disciples had gone away into the city to buy food. The Samaritan woman said to Jesus, "How is it that you, a Jewish man, ask a drink of me, a woman of Samaria?" For Judeans have no dealings with Samaritans. Jesus answered the woman, "If you knew the gift of God, and who it is that is saying to you, 'Give me a drink,' you would have asked him, and he would have given you living water." The woman said to him, "Sir, you have nothing to draw with, and the well is deep; where do you get that living water? Are you greater than our father Jacob, who gave us the well, and drank from it himself, and his children, and his cattle?" Jesus said to her, "Every one who drinks of this water will thirst again, but those who drink of the water that I shall give them will never thirst; the water that I shall give them will become in them a spring of water welling up to eternal life." The woman said to Jesus, "Sir, give me this water, that I may not thirst, nor come here to draw."

Jesus said to her, "Go, call your husband, and come here." The woman answered him, "I have no husband." Jesus said to her, "You are right in saying, 'I have no husband'; for you have had five husbands, and he whom you now have is not your husband; this you said truly." The woman said to Jesus, "Sir, I perceive that you are a prophet. Our forebears worshiped on this mountain; and you say that in Jerusalem is the place where it is proper to worship." Jesus said to her, "Woman, believe me, the hour is coming when neither on this mountain nor in Jerusalem will you worship the Father. You worship what you do not know; we worship what we know, for salvation is from the Jews. But the hour is coming, and now is, when the true worshipers will worship the Father in spirit and truth, for such worshipers the Father seeks. God is spirit, and those who worship God must worship in spirit and truth." The woman said to Jesus, "I know that Messiah is coming (the one who is called Christ); when that one comes, he will show us all things." [26]Jesus said to her, "I who speak to you am the one."

[27]Just then his disciples came. They marveled that Jesus was talking with a woman, but none said, "What do you wish?" or "Why are you talking with her?" So the woman left her water jar, and went away into the city, and said to the people, "Come, see someone who told me all that I ever did. Can this be the Christ?" They went out of the city and were coming to him.

Meanwhile the disciples besought Jesus, saying, "Rabbi, eat." But Jesus said to them, "I have food to eat of which you do not know." So the disciples said to one another, "Has any one brought him food?" Jesus said to them, "My food is to do the will and to accomplish the work of the one who sent me. Do you not say, 'There are yet four months, then comes the harvest?' I tell you, lift up your eyes, and see how the fields are already white for harvest. The reaper is already receiving wages, and gathers fruit for eternal life, so that the sower and reaper may rejoice together. For here the saying holds true, 'One sows and another reaps.' I sent you to reap that for which you did not labor; others have labored, and you have entered into their labor."

[39]Many Samaritans from that city believed in Jesus because of the woman's testimony, "He told me all that I ever did." So when the Samaritans came to him, they asked him to stay with them; and Jesus stayed there two days. And many more believed because of his word. [42]They said to the woman, "It is no longer because of your words that we believe, for we have heard for ourselves, and we know that this is indeed the Savior of the world."

L   John 9:1–41

[1]Passing by, Jesus saw someone who was blind from birth. And Jesus' disciples asked him, "Rabbi, who sinned, this person or his parents, that he was born blind?" Jesus answered, "It was not that this person sinned, or his parents, but that the works of God might be made manifest in him. We must work the works of the one who sent me, while it is day; night comes, when no one can work. As long as I am in the world, I am the light of the world." Saying this, Jesus spat on the ground and made clay of the spittle and anointed the man's eyes with the clay, saying to him, "Go, wash in the pool of Siloam" (which means Sent). So he went and washed and came back seeing. The neighbors and those who had seen him before as a beggar, said, "Is not this the person who used to sit and beg?" Some said, "It is he"; others said, "No, but he is like him." He said, "I am the one." They said to him, "Then how were your eyes opened?" He answered, "The man called Jesus made clay and anointed my eyes and said to me, 'Go to Siloam and wash'; so I went and washed and received my sight." They said to him, "Where is he?" He said, "I do not know."

They brought to the Pharisees the one who had formerly been blind. Now it was a sabbath day when Jesus made the clay and opened his eyes. The Pharisees again asked him how he had received his sight. And he said to them, "He put clay on my eyes, and I washed, and I see." Some of the Pharisees said, "This man is not from God, for he does not keep the sabbath." But others said, "How can a sinner do such signs?" There was a division among them. So they again said to the blind man, "What do you say about him, since he has opened your eyes?" He said, "He is a prophet."

The Jewish people did not believe that he had been blind and had received his sight, until they called the parents of the one who had received his sight, and asked them, "Is this your son, who you say was born blind? How then does he now see?" His parents answered, "We know that this is our son, and that he was born blind; but how he now sees we do not know, nor do we know who opened his eyes. Ask him; he is of age, he will speak for himself." His parents said this because they feared the Jewish people who had already agreed that any one confessing him to be Christ was to be put out of the synagogue. Therefore his parents said, "He is of age, ask him."

So for the second time they called the one who had been blind, and said to him, "Give God the praise; we know that this man is a sinner." He answered, "Whether he is a sinner, I do not know; one thing I know, that though I was blind, now I see." They said to him, "What did he do to you? How did he open your eyes?" He answered them, "I have told you already, and you would not listen. Why do you want to hear it again? Do you too want to become his disciples?" And they reviled him, saying, "You are his disciple, but we are disciples of Moses. We know that God has spoken to Moses, but as for this person, we do not know where he comes from." The man answered, "Why, this is a marvel! You do not know where he comes from, and yet he opened my eyes. We know that God does not listen to sinners, but God listens to any one who is devout and does God's will. Never since the world began has it been heard that any one opened the eyes of one born blind. If this person were not from God, he could do nothing." They answered him, "You were born in utter sin, and would you teach us?" And they cast him out.

Jesus heard that they had cast him out, and having found him, Jesus said, "Do you believe in the Man of Heaven?" He answered, "And who is the Man of Heaven, sir, that I may believe in him?" Jesus said to him, "You have seen him: the one speaking to you is the one." He said, "Lord, I believe"; and he worshiped Jesus. Jesus said, "For judgment I came into this world, that those who do not see may see, and that those who see may become blind." Some of the Pharisees near Jesus heard this, and they said to him, "Are we also blind?" [41]Jesus said to them, "If you were blind, you would have no guilt, but now that you say, 'We see,' your guilt remains."

FIRST READING

R 1 Samuel 16:1b, 6–7, 10–13a
E 1 Samuel 16:1–13

^{1a}The Lord said to Samuel, "How long will you grieve over Saul, seeing I have rejected him from being king over Israel? ^{1b}Fill your horn with oil, and go; I will send you to Jesse the Bethlehemite, for I have provided for myself a king among his sons." ²And Samuel said, "How can I go? If Saul hears it, he will kill me." And the Lord said, "Take a heifer with you, and say, 'I have come to sacrifice to the Lord.' And invite Jesse to the sacrifice, and I will show you what you shall do; and you shall anoint for me the one whom I name to you." Samuel did what the Lord commanded, and came to Bethlehem. The elders of the city came to meet him trembling, and said, "Do you come peaceably?" And Samuel said, "Peaceably; I have come to sacrifice to the Lord; consecrate yourselves, and come with me to the sacrifice." And he consecrated Jesse and his sons, and invited them to the sacrifice.

⁶When they came, Samuel looked on Eliab and thought, "Surely here before the Lord is the Lord's anointed one." ⁷But the Lord said to Samuel, "Do not look on his appearance or on the height of his stature, because I have rejected him; for the Lord sees beyond human sight; mortals look on the outward appearance, but the Lord looks on the heart." ⁸Then Jesse called Abinadab, and made him pass before Samuel. And he said, "Neither has the Lord chosen this one." Then Jesse made Shammah pass by. And Samuel said, "Neither has the Lord chosen this one." ¹⁰And Jesse made seven of his sons pass before Samuel. And Samuel said to Jesse, "The Lord has not chosen these." And Samuel said to Jesse, "Are all your sons here?" And Jesse said, "There remains yet the youngest, but behold, he is keeping the sheep." And Samuel said to Jesse, "Send and fetch him; for we will not sit down till he comes here." And he sent, and brought him in. Now he was ruddy, and had beautiful eyes, and was handsome. And the Lord

said, "Arise, anoint him; for this is the one." ¹³ᵃThen Samuel took the horn of oil, and anointed him in the midst of his brothers; and the Spirit of the LORD came mightily upon David from that day forward. ¹³ᵇAnd Samuel rose up, and went to Ramah.

L   Hosea 5:15–6:2

¹⁵I will return again to my place,
   until they acknowledge their guilt and seek my face,
   and in their distress they seek me, saying,
"Come, let us return to the LORD;
   for having torn, the LORD may heal us;
   having stricken, the LORD will bind us up.
²After two days the LORD will revive us;
   on the third day the LORD will raise us up,
   that we may live before the face of the LORD."

SECOND READING

R   E   Ephesians 5:8–14

⁸Once you were darkness, but now you are light in the Lord; walk as children of light (for the fruit of light is found in all that is good and right and true), and try to learn what is pleasing to the Lord. Take no part in the unfruitful works of darkness, but instead expose them. For it is a shame even to speak of the things that they do in secret; but when anything is exposed by the light it becomes visible, for anything that becomes visible is light. ¹⁴Therefore it is said,

"Awake, O sleeper, and arise from the dead,
and Christ shall give you light."

L   Romans 8:1–10

¹There is therefore now no condemnation for those who are in Christ Jesus. For the law of the Spirit of life in Christ Jesus has set me free from the law of sin and death. For God has done what the law, weakened by the flesh, could not do: sending God's own Son in the likeness of sinful flesh and for sin, God condemned sin in the flesh, in order that the just requirement of the law might be fulfilled in us, who walk not according to the flesh but according to the Spirit. For those who live accord-

ing to the flesh set their minds on the things of the flesh, but those who live according to the Spirit set their minds on the things of the Spirit. To set the mind on the flesh is death, but to set the mind on the Spirit is life and peace. For the mind that is set on the flesh is hostile to God; it does not submit to God's law, indeed it cannot; and those who are in the flesh cannot please God.

But you are not in the flesh, you are in the Spirit, if in fact the Spirit of God dwells in you. Any one who does not have the Spirit of Christ does not belong to Christ. ¹⁰But if Christ is in you, although your bodies are dead because of sin, your spirits are alive because of righteousness.

GOSPEL

R   John 9:1–41
E   John 9:1–13, 28–38

¹Passing by, Jesus saw someone who was blind from birth. And Jesus' disciples asked him, "Rabbi, who sinned, this person or his parents, that he was born blind?" Jesus answered, "It was not that this person sinned, or his parents, but that the works of God might be made manifest in him. We must work the works of the one who sent me, while it is day; night comes, when no one can work. As long as I am in the world, I am the light of the world." Saying this, Jesus spat on the ground and made clay of the spittle and anointed the man's eyes with the clay, saying to him, "Go, wash in the pool of Siloam" (which means Sent). So he went and washed and came back seeing. The neighbors and those who had seen him before as a beggar, said, "Is not this the person who used to sit and beg?" Some said, "It is he"; others said, "No, but he is like him." He said, "I am the one." They said to him, "Then how were your eyes opened?" He answered, "The man called Jesus made clay and anointed my eyes and said to me, 'Go to Siloam and wash'; so I went and washed and received my sight." They said to him, "Where is he?" He said, "I do not know."

¹³They brought to the Pharisees the one who had formerly been blind. ¹⁴Now it was a sabbath day when Jesus made the clay

and opened his eyes. The Pharisees again asked him how he had received his sight. And he said to them, "He put clay on my eyes, and I washed, and I see." Some of the Pharisees said, "This man is not from God, for he does not keep the sabbath." But others said, "How can a sinner do such signs?" There was a division among them. So they again said to the blind man, "What do you say about him, since he has opened your eyes?" He said, "He is a prophet."

The Jewish people did not believe that he had been blind and had received his sight, until they called the parents of the one who had received his sight, and asked them, "Is this your son, who you say was born blind? How then does he now see?" His parents answered, "We know that this is our son, and that he was born blind; but how he now sees we do not know nor do we know who opened his eyes. Ask him; he is of age, he will speak for himself." His parents said this because they feared the Jewish people who had already agreed that any one confessing him to be Christ was to be put out of the synagogue. Therefore his parents said, "He is of age, ask him."

So for the second time they called the one who had been blind, and said to him, "Give God the praise; we know that this man is a sinner." He answered, "Whether he is a sinner, I do not know; one thing I know, that though I was blind, now I see." They said to him, "What did he do to you? How did he open your eyes?" He answered them, "I have told you already, and you would not listen. Why do you want to hear it again? Do you too want to become his disciples?" [28]And they reviled him, saying, "You are his disciple, but we are disciples of Moses. We know that God has spoken to Moses, but as for this person, we do not know where he comes from." The man answered, "Why, this is a marvel! You do not know where he comes from, and yet he opened my eyes. We know that God does not listen to sinners, but God listens to any one who is devout and does God's will. Never since the world began has it been heard that any one opened the eyes of one born blind. If this person were not from God, he could do nothing." They answered him, "You were born in utter sin, and would you teach us?" And they cast him out.

Jesus heard that they had cast him out, and having found him, Jesus said, "Do you believe in the Man of Heaven?" He answered, "And who is the Man of Heaven, sir, that I may believe in him?" Jesus said to him, "You have seen him: the one speaking to you is the one." ³⁸He said, "Lord, I believe"; and he worshiped Jesus. ³⁹Jesus said, "For judgment I came into this world, that those who do not see may see, and that those who see may become blind." Some of the Pharisees near Jesus heard this, and they said to him, "Are we also blind?" ⁴¹Jesus said to them, "If you were blind, you would have no guilt; but now that you say, 'We see,' your guilt remains."

L   Matthew 20:17–28

¹⁷As Jesus was going up to Jerusalem, he took the twelve disciples aside, and on the way said to them, "Behold, we are going up to Jerusalem; and the Man of Heaven will be delivered to the chief priests and scribes, and they will condemn him to death, and deliver him to the Gentiles to be mocked and scourged and crucified, and he will be raised on the third day."

Then the mother of the sons of Zebedee came up to Jesus, with her sons, and kneeling before him she asked him for something. And Jesus said to her, "What do you want?" She said to him, "Command that these two sons of mine may sit, one at your right hand and one at your left, in your dominion." But Jesus answered, "You do not know what you are asking. Are you able to drink the cup that I am to drink?" They said to him, "We are able." Jesus said to them, "You will drink my cup, but to sit at my right hand and at my left is not mine to grant, but it is for those for whom it has been prepared by my Father." And when the ten heard it, they were indignant at the two brothers. But Jesus called them to him and said, "You know that the rulers of the Gentiles are domineering, and their mighty ones exercise authority over them. It shall not be so among you; but whoever would be great among you must be your servant, and whoever would be first among you must be your slave; ²⁸even as the Man of Heaven came not to be served but to serve, and to give his life as a ransom for many."

R E L FIFTH SUNDAY IN LENT

FIRST READING

R   Ezekiel 37:12–14
E L   Ezekiel 37:1–3, 11–14

[1]The hand of the LORD was upon me, and brought me out by the Spirit of the LORD, and set me down in the midst of the valley; it was full of bones. And the LORD led me round among them; and behold, there were very many upon the valley; and lo, they were very dry. [3]And the LORD said to me, "O human one, can these bones live?" And I answered, "O Lord GOD, you know."

[11]Then the LORD said to me, "O human one, these bones are the whole house of Israel. Behold, they say, 'Our bones are dried up, and our hope is lost; we are clean cut off.' [12]Therefore prophesy, and say to them, Thus says the Lord GOD: Behold, I will open your graves, and raise you from your graves, O my people; and I will bring you home into the land of Israel. And you shall know that I am the LORD, when I open your graves, and raise you from your graves, O my people. [14]And I will put my Spirit within you, and you shall live, and I will place you in your own land; then you shall know that I, the LORD, have spoken, and I have done it, says the LORD."

SECOND READING

R   Romans 8:8–11
L   Romans 8:11–19

[8]Those who are in the flesh cannot please God.

But you are not in the flesh, you are in the Spirit, if in fact the Spirit of God dwells in you. Any one who does not have the Spirit of Christ does not belong to Christ. But if Christ is in you, although your bodies are dead because of sin, your spirits are alive because of righteousness. [11]If the Spirit of the one who raised Jesus from the dead dwells in you, the one who raised Christ Jesus from the dead will give life to your mortal bodies also through this Spirit dwelling in you.

¹²So then, my dear people, we are debtors, not to the flesh, to live according to the flesh—for if you live according to the flesh you will die, but if by the Spirit you put to death the deeds of the body you will live. For all who are led by the Spirit of God are children of God. For you did not receive the spirit of slavery to fall back into fear, but you have received the spirit of adoption. When we cry, "Abba! Father!" it is that very Spirit bearing witness with our spirit that we are children of God, and if children, then heirs, heirs of God and joint heirs with Christ, provided we suffer with Christ in order that we may also be glorified with Christ.

I consider that the sufferings of this present time are not worth comparing with the glory that is to be revealed to us. ¹⁹For the creation waits with eager longing for the revealing of the children of God.

E   Romans 6:16–23

¹⁶Do you not know that if you yield yourselves to any one as obedient slaves, you are slaves of the one whom you obey, either of sin, which leads to death, or of obedience, which leads to righteousness? But thanks be to God, that you who were once slaves of sin have become obedient from the heart to the standard of teaching to which you were committed, and, having been set free from sin, have become slaves of righteousness. I am speaking in human terms, because of your natural limitations. For just as you once yielded your physical bodies to impurity and to greater and greater iniquity, so now yield your physical bodies to righteousness for sanctification.

When you were slaves of sin, you were free in regard to righteousness. But then what return did you get from the things of which you are now ashamed? The end of those things is death. But now that you have been set free from sin and have become slaves of God, the return you get is sanctification and its end, eternal life. ²³For the wages of sin is death, but the free gift of God is eternal life in Christ Jesus our Lord.

GOSPEL

R John 11:1–45
E John 11:18–44
L John 11:1–53

¹Now a certain man was ill, Lazarus of Bethany, the village of Mary and her sister Martha. It was Mary who anointed the Lord with ointment and wiped his feet with her hair, whose brother Lazarus was ill. So the sisters sent to Jesus, saying, "Lord, he whom you love is ill." But when Jesus heard it he said, "This illness is not unto death; it is for the glory of God, so that the Son of God may be glorified by means of it."

Now Jesus loved Martha and her sister and Lazarus. So when Jesus heard that Lazarus was ill, he stayed two days longer in the place where he was. Then after this he said to the disciples, "Let us go into Judea again." The disciples said to him, "Rabbi, the Judeans were but now seeking to stone you, and are you going there again?" Jesus answered, "Are there not twelve hours in the day? Those who walk in the day do not stumble because they see the light of this world. But those who walk in the night do stumble, because the light is not in them." Thus Jesus spoke, and then said to them, "Our friend Lazarus has fallen asleep, but I go to awake him out of sleep." The disciples said to him, "Lord, if he has fallen asleep, he will recover." Now Jesus had spoken of his death, but they thought that he meant taking rest in sleep. Then Jesus told them plainly, "Lazarus is dead; and for your sake I am glad that I was not there, so that you may believe. But let us go to him." Thomas, called the Twin, said to the other disciples, "Let us also go, that we may die with him."

Now when Jesus came, he found that Lazarus had already been in the tomb four days. ¹⁸Bethany was near Jerusalem, about two miles off, and many of the Judeans had come to Martha and Mary to console them concerning their brother. When Martha heard that Jesus was coming, she went and met him, while Mary sat in the house. Martha said to Jesus, "Lord, if you had been here, my brother would not have died. And even now I know that whatever you ask from God, God will give you." Jesus said to her, "Your brother will rise again." Martha said to Jesus, "I know that he will rise again in the resurrection at the last day." Jesus said to her, "I am the resurrection and the life; they who believe in me, though they die, yet shall they live, and whoever lives and believes in me shall never die. Do you believe this?" She said to him, "Yes, Lord; I believe that you are the Christ, the Son of God, the one who is coming into the world."

Having said this, Martha went and called her sister Mary, saying quietly, "The Teacher is here and is calling for you." And when Mary heard it, she rose quickly and went to him. Now Jesus had not yet come to the village, but was still in the place where Martha had met him. When the Jewish people who were with her in the house, consoling her, saw Mary rise quickly and go out, they followed her, supposing that she was going to the tomb to weep there. Then Mary, when she came where Jesus was and saw him, fell at his feet, saying to him, "Lord, if you had been here, my brother would not have died." When Jesus saw her weeping, and the Jewish people who came with her also weeping, he was deeply moved in spirit and troubled; and Jesus said, "Where have you laid him?" They said to him, "Lord, come and see." Jesus wept. So the Jewish people said, "See how he loved him!" But some of them said, "Could not the one who opened the eyes of the blind man have kept this man from dying?"

Then Jesus, deeply moved again, came to the tomb; it was a cave, and a stone lay upon it. Jesus said, "Take away the stone." Martha, the sister of the deceased, said to Jesus, "Lord, by this time there will be an odor, for he has been dead four days." Jesus said to her, "Did I not tell you that if you would believe you would see the glory of God?" So they took away the stone. And Jesus lifted up his eyes and said, "Father, I thank you that you have heard me. I knew that you hear me always, but I have said this on account of the people standing by, that they may believe that you sent me." Having said this, Jesus cried with a loud voice, "Lazarus, come out." [44]The dead man came out, his hands and feet bound with bandages, and his face wrapped with a cloth. Jesus said to them, "Unbind him, and let him go."

45Many of the Judeans therefore, who had come with Mary and had seen what Jesus did, believed in him; 46but some of them went to the Pharisees and told them what Jesus had done. So the chief priests and the Pharisees gathered the council, and said, "What are we to do? For this person performs many signs. If we let him go on thus, every one will believe in him, and the Romans will come and destroy both our holy place and our nation." But one of them, Caiaphas, who was high priest that year, said to them, "You know nothing at all; you do not understand that it is expedient for you that one person should die for the people, and that the whole nation should not perish." He did not say this of his own accord, but being high priest that year he prophesied that Jesus should die for the nation, and not for the nation only, but to gather into one the children of God who are scattered abroad. 53So from that day on they took counsel how to put Jesus to death.

R E L   LITURGY OF THE PALMS

R E L   Matthew 21:1–11

¹When the crowd drew near to Jerusalem and came to Beth-phage, to the Mount of Olives, then Jesus sent two disciples, saying to them, "Go into the village opposite you, and immediately you will find a donkey tied, and a colt with her; untie them and bring them to me. If any one says anything to you, you shall say, 'The Lord has need of them,' and they will be sent immediately." This took place to fulfill what was spoken by the prophet, saying,

"Tell the daughter of Zion,
Behold, your king is coming to you,
humble, and mounted on a donkey,
and on a colt, the foal of a donkey."

The disciples went and did as Jesus had directed them; they brought the donkey and the colt, and put their garments on them, and he sat thereon. Most of the crowd spread their garments on the road, and others cut branches from the trees and spread them on the road. And the crowds that went before and that followed shouted, "Hosanna to the Son of David! Blessed is the one who comes in the name of the Lord! Hosanna in the highest!" And when Jesus entered Jerusalem, all the city was stirred, saying, "Who is this!" ¹¹And the crowds said, "This is the prophet Jesus from Nazareth of Galilee."

FIRST READING

R   Isaiah 50:4–7
L   Isaiah 50:4–9a

[4]The Lord GOD has given me
   the tongue of those who are taught,
that I may know how to sustain with a word
   those who are weary.
Morning by morning the Lord GOD wakens,
   wakens my ear,
   to hear as those who are taught.
The Lord GOD has opened my ear,
   and I was not rebellious,
   I turned not backward.
I gave my back to the smiters,
   and my cheeks to those who pulled out the beard;
I hid not my face
   from shame and spitting.
[7]For the Lord GOD helps me;
   therefore I have not been confounded;
therefore I have set my face like a flint,
   and I know that I shall not be put to shame;
   [8]the one who vindicates me is near.
Who will contend with me?
   Let us stand up together.
Who is my adversary?
   Let my adversary come near to me.
[9a]Behold, the Lord GOD helps me;
   who will declare me guilty?

E   Isaiah 45:21–25

[21]"Declare and present your case;
   let them take counsel together!
Who told this long ago?
   Who declared it of old?
Was it not I, the LORD?
   And there is no other god besides me,

a righteous God and a Savior;
  there is none besides me.
Turn to me and be saved,
  all the ends of the earth!
  For I am God, and there is no other.
By myself I have sworn,
  from my mouth has gone forth in righteousness
  a word that shall not return:
'To me every knee shall bow,
  every tongue shall swear.'
Only in the LORD, it shall be said of me,
  are righteousness and strength;
to the LORD shall come and be ashamed,
  all who were incensed against God.
²⁵In the LORD all the offspring of Israel
  shall triumph and glory."

SECOND READING

R Philippians 2:6–11
E L Philippians 2:5–11

⁵Have this mind among yourselves, which is yours in Christ
Jesus, ⁶who, being in the form of God, did not count equality
with God a thing to be grasped, but gave it up, taking the form
of a servant, being born in human likeness. And being found
in human form he humbled himself and became obedient unto
death, even death on a cross. Therefore God has highly exalted
him and bestowed on him the name which is above every
name, that at the name of Jesus every knee should bow, in
heaven and on earth and under the earth, ¹¹and every tongue
confess that Jesus Christ is Lord, to the glory of God, the
Father.

GOSPEL

R   Matthew 26:14–27:66
E   Matthew 27:1–54
L   Matthew 26:1–27:66

Speaking parts:

Narrator
Jesus
Speaker: Judas, Peter, High Priest, Maid, Another Maid, Pilate,
   People

Narrator:
¹When Jesus had finished all these sayings, he said to his
disciples,

Jesus:
You know that after two days the Passover is coming, and the
Man of Heaven will be delivered up to be crucified.

Narrator:
Then the chief priests and the elders of the people gathered in
the palace of the high priest, who was called Caiaphas, and
took counsel together in order to arrest Jesus by stealth and kill
him. But they said,

People:
Not during the feast, lest there be a tumult among the people.

Narrator:
Now when Jesus was at Bethany in the house of Simon the
leper, a woman came up to him with an alabaster flask of very
expensive ointment, and she poured it on his head, as he sat at
table. But when the disciples saw it, they were indignant,
saying,

People:
Why this waste? For this ointment might have been sold for a
large sum, and given to the poor.

Narrator:
Jesus, aware of this, said to them,

Jesus:
Why do you trouble the woman? For she has done a beautiful

thing to me. For you always have the poor with you, but you will not always have me. In pouring this ointment on my body she has done it to prepare me for burial. Truly, I say to you, wherever this gospel is preached in the whole world, what she has done will be told in memory of her.

Narrator:
[14]Then one of the twelve, who was called Judas Iscariot, went to the chief priests and said,

Judas:
What will you give me if I deliver Jesus to you?

Narrator:
And they paid him thirty pieces of silver. And from that moment Judas sought an opportunity to betray him.

Now on the first day of Unleavened Bread the disciples came to Jesus, saying,

People:
Where will you have us prepare for you to eat the passover?

Narrator:
Jesus said,

Jesus:
Go into the city, and say to a certain one, "The Teacher says, My time is at hand; I will keep the passover at your house with my disciples."

Narrator:
And the disciples did as Jesus had directed them, and they prepared the passover.

When it was evening, he sat at table with the twelve disciples; and as they were eating, he said,

Jesus:
Truly, I say to you, one of you will betray me.

Narrator:
And they were very sorrowful, and began to say to him one after another,

People:
Is it I, Lord?

Narrator:
Jesus answered,

Jesus:
The one who has dipped his hand in the dish with me, will betray me. The Man of Heaven goes as it is written of him, but woe to that person by whom the Man of Heaven is betrayed! It would have been better for that person never to have been born.

Narrator:
Judas, who betrayed him, said,

Judas:
Is it I, Master?

Narrator:
Jesus said to him,

Jesus:
You have said so.

Narrator:
Now as they were eating, Jesus took bread, and blessed, and broke it, and gave it to the disciples and said,

Jesus:
Take, eat; this is my body.

Narrator:
And he took a cup, and having given thanks he gave it to them saying,

Jesus:
Drink of it, all of you; for this is my blood of the covenant, which is poured out for many for the forgiveness of sins. I tell you I shall not drink again of this fruit of the vine until that day when I drink it new with you in the dominion of my Father.

Narrator:
And when they had sung a hymn, they went out to the Mount of Olives. Then Jesus said to them,

Jesus:
You will all fall away because of me this night; for it is written, "I will strike the shepherd, and the sheep of the flock will be

scattered." But after I am raised up, I will go before you to Galilee.

Narrator:
Peter declared to him,

Peter:
Though they all fall away because of you, I will never fall away.

Narrator:
Jesus said to him,

Jesus:
Truly, I say to you, this very night, before the cock crows, you will deny me three times.

Narrator:
Peter said to him,

Peter:
Even if I must die with you, I will not deny you.

Narrator:
And so said all the disciples. Then Jesus went with them to a place called Gethsemane, and he said to his disciples,

Jesus:
Sit here, while I go yonder and pray.

Narrator:
And taking along Peter and the two sons of Zebedee, Jesus began to be sorrowful and troubled. Then he said to them,

Jesus:
My soul is very sorrowful, even to death; remain here, and watch with me.

Narrator:
And going a little farther he fell on his face and prayed,

Jesus:
My Father, if it be possible, let this cup pass from me; nevertheless, not as I will, but as you will.

Narrator:
And Jesus came to the disciples and found them sleeping; and he said to Peter,

Jesus:

So, could you not watch with me one hour? Watch and pray that you may not enter into temptation; the spirit indeed is willing, but the flesh is weak.

Narrator:

Again, for the second time, Jesus went away and prayed,

Jesus:

My Father, if this cannot pass unless I drink it, your will be done.

Narrator:

And again Jesus came and found them sleeping, for their eyes were heavy. So, leaving them again, he went away and prayed for the third time, saying the same words. Then Jesus came to the disciples and said to them,

Jesus:

Are you still sleeping and taking your rest? Behold, the hour is at hand, and the Man of Heaven is betrayed into the hands of sinners. Rise, let us be going; see, my betrayer is at hand.

Narrator:

While he was still speaking, Judas came, one of the twelve, and with him a great crowd with swords and clubs, from the chief priests and the elders of the people. Now the betrayer had given them a sign, saying,

Judas:

Whomever I shall kiss is the one; seize him.

Narrator:

And he came up to Jesus at once and said,

Judas:

Hail, Master!

Narrator:

And he kissed him. Jesus said to him,

Jesus:

Friend, why are you here?

Narrator:

Then they came up and laid hands on Jesus and seized him.

And behold, one of those who were with Jesus stretched out his hand and drew his sword, and struck the slave of the high priest, and cut off his ear. Then Jesus said to him,

Jesus:
Put your sword back into its place; for all who take the sword will perish by the sword. Do you think that I cannot appeal to my Father who will at once send me more than twelve legions of angels? But how then should the scriptures be fulfilled, that it must be so?

Narrator:
At that hour Jesus said to the crowds,

Jesus:
Have you come out as against a robber, with swords and clubs to capture me? Day after day I sat in the temple teaching, and you did not seize me. But all this has taken place, that the scriptures of the prophets might be fulfilled.

Narrator:
Then all the disciples forsook him and fled.

Then those who had seized Jesus led him to Caiaphas the high priest, where the scribes and the elders had gathered. But Peter followed him at a distance, as far as the courtyard of the high priest, and going inside he sat with the guards to see the end. Now the chief priests and the whole council sought false testimony against Jesus that they might put him to death, but they found none, though many false witnesses came forward. At last two came forward and said,

People:
This man said, "I am able to destroy the temple of God, and to build it in three days."

Narrator:
And the high priest stood up and said,

High Priest:
Have you no answer to make? What is it that these people testify against you?

Narrator:
But Jesus was silent. And the high priest said to him,

High Priest:

I adjure you by the living God, tell us if you are the Christ, the
Son of God.

Narrator:

Jesus said to him,

Jesus:

You have said so. But I tell you, hereafter you will see the Man
of Heaven seated at the right hand of Power, and coming on
the clouds of heaven.

Narrator:

Then the high priest tore his robes, and said,

High Priest:

He has uttered blasphemy. Why do we still need witnesses?
You have now heard his blasphemy. What is your judgment?

Narrator:

They answered,

People:

He deserves death.

Narrator:

Then they spat in his face, and struck him; and some slapped
him, saying,

People:

Prophesy to us, you Christ! Who is it that struck you?

Narrator:

Now Peter was sitting outside in the courtyard. And a maid
came up to him, and said,

Maid:

You also were with Jesus the Galilean.

Narrator:

But he denied it before them all, saying,

Peter:

I do not know what you mean.

Narrator:

And when he went out to the porch, another maid saw him,
and she said to the bystanders,

Another Maid:
This man was with Jesus of Nazareth.

Narrator:
And again he denied it with an oath,

Peter:
I do not know the man.

Narrator:
After a little while the bystanders came up and said to Peter,

People:
Certainly you are also one of them, for your accent betrays you.

Narrator:
Then he began to invoke a curse on himself and to swear,

Peter:
I do not know the man.

Narrator:
And immediately the cock crowed. And Peter remembered the saying of Jesus, "Before the cock crows, you will deny me three times." And he went out and wept bitterly.

When morning came, all the chief priests and the elders of the people took counsel against Jesus to put him to death; and they bound him and led him away and delivered him to Pilate the governor.

When Judas, his betrayer, saw that Jesus was condemned, he repented and brought back the thirty pieces of silver to the chief priests and the elders, saying,

Judas:
I have sinned in betraying innocent blood.

Narrator:
They said,

People:
What is that to us? See to it yourself.

Narrator:
And throwing down the pieces of silver in the temple, he departed; and he went and hanged himself. But the chief priests, taking the pieces of silver, said,

People:

It is not lawful to put them into the treasury, since they are blood money.

Narrator:

So they took counsel, and bought with them the potter's field, to bury strangers in. Therefore that field has been called the Field of Blood to this day. Then was fulfilled what had been spoken by the prophet Jeremiah, saying, "And they took the thirty pieces of silver, the price of the one on whom a price had been set by some of the Israelites, and they gave them for the potter's field, as the Lord directed me."

Now Jesus stood before the governor; and the governor asked him,

Pilate:

Are you the King of the Jews?

Narrator:

Jesus said,

Jesus:

You have said so.

Narrator:

But when Jesus was accused by the chief priests and elders, he made no answer. Then Pilate said to him,

Pilate:

Do you not hear how many things they testify against you?

Narrator:

But Jesus gave Pilate no answer, not even to a single charge; so that the governor wondered greatly.

Now at the feast the governor was accustomed to release for the crowd any one prisoner whom they wanted. And they had then a notorious prisoner, called Barabbas. So when they gathered, Pilate said to them,

Pilate:

Whom do you want me to release for you, Barabbas or Jesus who is called Christ?

Narrator:
For Pilate knew that it was out of envy that they had delivered him up. Besides, while he was sitting on the judgment seat, his wife sent words to him. "Have nothing to do with that right-eous man, for I have suffered much over him today in a dream." Now the chief priests and the elders persuaded the people to ask for Barabbas and destroy Jesus. The government again said to them,

Pilate:
Which of the two do you want me to release for you?

Narrator:
And they said,

People:
Barabbas.

Narrator:
Pilate said to them,

Pilate:
Then what shall I do with Jesus who is called Christ?

Narrator:
They all said,

People:
Let him be crucified.

Narrator:
And Pilate said,

Pilate:
Why, what evil has he done?

Narrator:
But they shouted all the more,

People:
Let him be crucified.

Narrator:
So when Pilate saw that he was gaining nothing, but rather that a riot was beginning, he took water and washed his hands before the crowd, saying,

Pilate:
I am innocent of this man's blood, see to it yourselves.

Narrator:
And all the people answered,

People:
His blood be on us and on our children!

Narrator:
Then Pilate released for them Barabbas, and having scourged Jesus, delivered him to be crucified. Then the soldiers of the governor took Jesus into the praetorium, and they gathered the whole battalion before him. And they stripped him and put a scarlet robe upon him, and plaiting a crown of thorns they put it on his head, and put a reed in his right hand. And kneeling before him they mocked him, saying,

People:
Hail, King of the Jews!

Narrator:
And they spat upon him, and took the reed and struck him on the head. And when they had mocked him, they stripped him of the robe, and put his own clothes on him, and led him away to crucify him.

As they went out, they came upon a Cyrenean, Simon by name, whom they compelled to carry his cross. And when they came to the place called Golgotha (which means the place of a skull), they offered him wine to drink, mingled with gall; but when he tasted it, he would not drink it. And when they had crucified him, they divided his garments among them by casting lots; then they sat down and kept watch over him there. And over his head they put the charge against him, which read, "This is Jesus the King of the Jews." Then two robbers were crucified with him, one on the right and one on the left. And those who passed by derided him, wagging their heads and saying,

People:
You who would destroy the temple and build it in three days, save yourself! If you are the Son of God, come down from the cross.

Narrator:
So also the chief priests, with the scribes and elders, mocked him, saying,

People:
He who saved others cannot save himself. Let the King of Israel come down now from the cross, and we will believe in him. He trusts in God; let God deliver him now, if God desires him; for he said, "I am the Son of God."

Narrator:
And the robbers who were crucified with him also reviled him in the same way.

Now from the sixth hour there was darkness over all the land until the ninth hour. And about the ninth hour Jesus cried out with a loud voice,

Jesus:
Eli, Eli, lama sabach-thani?

Narrator:
That is, "My God, my God, why have you forsaken me?" And some of the bystanders hearing it said,

People:
He is calling Elijah.

Narrator:
And one of them at once ran and took a sponge, filled it with vinegar, and put it on a reed, and gave it to him to drink. But the others said,

People:
Wait, let us see whether Elijah will come to save him.

Narrator:
And Jesus cried again with a loud voice and yielded up his spirit.

And behold, the curtain of the temple was torn in two, from top to bottom; and the earth shook, and the rocks were split; the tombs also were opened, and many bodies of the saints who had fallen asleep were raised, and coming out of the tombs after Jesus' resurrection they went into the holy city and appeared to many. [54]When the centurion and those who were with him, keeping watch over Jesus, saw the earthquake and what took place, they were filled with awe, and said,

People:
Truly this was the Son of God!

Narrator:
[55]There were also many women there, looking on from afar, who had followed Jesus from Galilee, ministering to him; among whom were Mary Magdalene, and Mary the mother of James and Joseph, and the mother of the sons of Zebedee. When it was evening, there came a rich man from Arimathea, named Joseph, who also was a disciple of Jesus. He went to Pilate and asked for the body of Jesus. Then Pilate ordered it to be given to him. And Joseph took the body, wrapped it in a clean linen shroud, and laid it in his own new tomb, which he had hewn in the rock; and he rolled a great stone to the door of the tomb, and departed. Mary Magdalene and the other Mary were there, sitting opposite the sepulchre.

Next day, that is, after the day of Preparation, the chief priests and the Pharisees gathered before Pilate and said,

People:
Sir, we remember how that imposter said, while he was still alive, "After three days I will rise again." Therefore order the sepulchre to be made secure until the third day, lest his disciples go and steal him away, and tell the people, "He has risen from the dead," and the last fraud will be worse than the first.

Narrator:
Pilate said to them,

Pilate:
You have a guard of soldiers; go, make it as secure as you can.

Narrator:
[66]So they went and made the sepulchre secure by sealing the stone and setting a guard.

R HOLY THURSDAY
E L MAUNDY THURSDAY

FIRST READING

R   Exodus 12:1–8, 11–14
E   Exodus 12:1–14a
L   Exodus 12:1–14

¹The LORD said to Moses and Aaron in the land of Egypt, "This month shall be for you the beginning of months; it shall be the first month of the year for you. Tell all the congregation of Israel that on the tenth day of this month they shall take every man a lamb according to their fathers' houses, a lamb for a household; and if the household is too small for a lamb, then a man and his neighbor next to his house shall take according to the number of persons; according to what each can eat you shall make your count for the lamb. Your lamb shall be without blemish, a male a year old; you shall take it from the sheep or from the goats; and you shall keep it until the fourteenth day of this month, when the whole assembly of the congregation of Israel shall kill their lambs in the evening. Then they shall take some of the blood, and put it on the two doorposts and the lintel of the houses in which they eat them. ⁸They shall eat the flesh that night, roasted; with unleavened bread and bitter herbs they shall eat it. ⁹Do not eat any of it raw or boiled with water, but roasted, its head with its legs and its inner parts. And you shall let none of it remain until the morning, anything that remains until the morning you shall burn. ¹¹In this manner you shall eat it: your loins girded, your sandals on your feet, and your staff in your hand; and you shall eat it in haste. It is the LORD's passover. For I will pass through the land of Egypt that night, and I will smite all the first-born in the land of Egypt, both human and animal; and on all the gods of Egypt I will execute judgments: I am the LORD. The blood shall be a sign for you, upon the houses where you are; and when I see the blood, I will pass over you, and no plague shall fall upon you to destroy you, when I smite the land of Egypt.

14a"This day shall be for you a memorial day, and you shall keep it as a feast to the LORD; 14bthroughout your generations you shall observe it as an ordinance for ever."

SECOND READING

R E   1 Corinthians 11:23–26
   L   1 Corinthians 11:17–32

17In the following instructions I do not commend you, because when you come together it is not for the better but for the worse. For, in the first place, when you assemble as a church, I hear that there are divisions among you; and I partly believe it, for there must be factions among you in order that those who are genuine among you may be recognized. When you meet together, it is not the Lord's supper that you eat. For in eating, each of you goes ahead with your own meal, and one is hungry and another is drunk. What! Do you not have houses to eat and drink in? Or do you despise the church of God and humiliate those who have nothing? What shall I say to you? Shall I commend you in this? No, I will not.

23For I received from the Lord what I also delivered to you, that the Lord Jesus on the night when he was betrayed took bread, and having given thanks, broke it, and said, "This is my body which is for you. Do this in remembrance of me." In the same way also the cup, after supper, saying, "This cup is the new covenant in my blood. Do this, as often as you drink it, in remembrance of me." 26For as often as you eat this bread and drink the cup, you proclaim the Lord's death until he comes.

27Whoever, therefore, eats the bread or drinks the cup of the Lord in an unworthy manner will be guilty of profaning the body and blood of the Lord. Examine yourselves, and so eat of the bread and drink of the cup. For all who eat and drink without discerning the body eat and drink judgment upon themselves. That is why many of you are weak and ill, and some have died. But if we judged ourselves truly, we should not be judged. 32But when we are judged by the Lord, we are chastened so that we may not be condemned along with the world.

GOSPEL

R E John 13:1–15
   L John 13:1–17, 34

¹Now before the feast of the Passover, when Jesus knew that his hour had come to depart out of this world to the Father, having loved his own who were in the world, he loved them to the end. And during supper, when the devil had already put it into the heart of Judas Iscariot, Simon's son, to betray him, Jesus, knowing that the Father had given all things into his hands, and that he had come from God and was going to God, rose from supper, laid aside his garments, and girded himself with a towel. Then he poured water into a basin, and began to wash the disciples' feet, and to wipe them with the towel with which he was girded. Jesus came to Simon Peter; and Peter said to him, "Lord, do you wash my feet?" Jesus answered him, "What I am doing you do not know now, but afterward you will understand." Peter said to him, "You shall never wash my feet." Jesus answered Peter, "If I do not wash you, you have no part in me." Simon Peter said to Jesus, "Lord, not my feet only but also my hands and my head!" Jesus said to him, "Those who have bathed do not need to wash, except for their feet, but they are clean all over; and you are clean, but not every one of you." For Jesus knew who was to betray him; that was why he said, "You are not all clean."

When Jesus had washed their feet, and taken his garments, and resumed his place, he said to them, "Do you know what I have done to you? You call me Teacher and Lord; and you are right, for so I am. If I then, your Lord and Teacher, have washed your feet, you also ought wash one another's feet. ¹⁵For I have given you an example, that you should do as I have done to you. ¹⁶Truly, truly, I say to you, slaves are not greater than their masters; nor those who are sent greater than the one who sent them. ¹⁷If you know these things, blessed are you if you do them.

³⁴"A new commandment. I give to you, that you love one another; even as I have loved you, that you also love one another."

R E L GOOD FRIDAY

FIRST READING

R E L   Isaiah 52:13–53:12

¹³Behold, my servant shall prosper,
   shall be exalted and lifted up,
   and shall be very high.
As many were astonished at the one
   whose appearance was so marred, beyond human
     semblance,
   and whose form was beyond that of humankind,
so shall my servant startle many nations;
   rulers shall shut their mouths because of him;
for that which has not been told them they shall see,
   and that which they have not heard they shall understand.
Who has believed what we have heard?
   And to whom has the arm of the LORD been revealed?
For the servant grew up before the LORD like a young plant,
   and like a root out of dry ground,
having no form or comeliness for us to behold,
   and no beauty for us to desire.
He was despised and rejected by men,
   a man of sorrows, and acquainted with grief;
and as one from whom people hid their faces,
   he was despised, and we esteemed him not.
Surely he has borne our griefs
   and carried our sorrows;
yet we esteemed him stricken,
   smitten by God, and afflicted.
But he was wounded for our transgressions,
   and was bruised for our iniquities;
the chastisement that made us whole was upon him,
   by whose stripes we are healed.
All we like sheep have gone astray;
   we have turned each one to our own way,
and the LORD has laid on this servant
   the iniquity of us all.

This servant was oppressed and was afflicted,
  yet opened not his mouth;
like a lamb that is led to the slaughter,
  and like a ewe that before her shearers is dumb,
  so he opened not his mouth.
By oppression and judgment the servant was taken away;
  and as for his generation, who considered
that he was cut off out of the land of the living,
  stricken for the transgression of my people?
He was given a grave with the wicked,
  and was with the rich in death,
although having done no violence,
  having never spoken deceit.
Yet it was the will of the Lord to bruise this servant;
  the Lord has put him to grief;
making himself an offering for sin,
  the servant shall see offspring and shall prolong his days;
the will of the Lord shall prosper in the hand of the servant,
  who shall see the fruit of the travail of his soul and be
    satisfied;
by his knowledge shall the righteous one, my servant,
  make many to be accounted righteous;
  my servant shall bear their iniquities.
12Therefore I will divide a portion with the great for my servant
  who shall divide the spoil with the strong;
because my servant poured out his soul to death,
  and was numbered with the transgressors;
yet he bore the sin of many,
  and made intercession for the transgressors.

SECOND READING

R L   Hebrews 4:14–16, 5:7–9

14Since then we have a great high priest who has passed
through the heavens, Jesus, the Son of God, let us hold fast
our confession. For we have not a high priest who is unable to
sympathize with our weaknesses, but one who in every respect
has been tempted as we are, yet without sin. 16Let us then with

confidence draw near to the throne of grace, that we may receive mercy and find grace to help in time of need.

[7]In the days of his flesh, Jesus offered up prayers and supplications, with loud cries and tears, to the one who was able to save him from death, and for being God-fearing Jesus was heard. Although being a Son, Jesus learned obedience through what he suffered; [9]and being made perfect Jesus became the source of eternal salvation to all who obey him.

E   Hebrews 10:1–25

[1]For since the law has but a shadow of the good things to come instead of the true form of these realities, it can never, by the same sacrifices which are continually offered year after year, make perfect those who draw near. Otherwise, would they not have ceased to be offered? If the worshipers had once been cleansed, they would no longer have any consciousness of sin. But in these sacrifices there is a reminder of sin year after year. For it is impossible that the blood of bulls and goats should take away sins.

Consequently, coming into the world, Christ said,

"Sacrifices and offerings you have not desired,
but a body you have prepared for me;
in burnt offerings and sin offerings you have taken no
     pleasure.
Then I said, 'Lo, I have come to do your will, O God,'
as it is written of me in the roll of the book."

When Christ said above, "You have neither desired nor taken pleasure in sacrifices and offerings and burnt offerings and sin offerings" (these are offered according to the law), then Christ added, "Lo, I have come to do your will." Christ abolishes the first in order to establish the second. And by that will we have been sanctified through the offering of the body of Jesus Christ once for all.

And every priest stands at the daily service, offering repeatedly the same sacrifices, which can never take away sins. But when Christ had offered for all time a single sacrifice for sins, he sat down at the right hand of God, then to wait until his enemies should be made a stool for his feet. For by a single offering Christ has perfected for all time those who are sanctified. And the Holy Spirit also bears witness to us; for after saying,

"This is the covenant that I will make with them
after those days, says the Lord:
I will put my laws on their hearts, and write them on their
   minds,"

then is added,

"I will remember their sins and their misdeeds no more."

Where there is forgiveness of these, there is no longer any offering for sin.

Therefore, my dear people, since we have confidence to enter the sanctuary by the blood of Jesus, by the new and living way which Christ opened for us through the curtain, that is, through his flesh, and since we have a great priest over the house of God, let us draw near with a true heart in full assurance of faith, with our hearts sprinkled clean from an evil conscience and our bodies washed with pure water. Let us hold fast the confession of our hope without wavering, for the one who promised is faithful; and let us consider how to stir up one another to love and good works, ²⁵not neglecting to meet together, as is the habit of some, but encouraging one another, and all the more as you see the Day drawing near.

GOSPEL

R L   John 18:1–19:42
   E   John 19:1–37

Narrator
Jesus
Speaker: Maid, Peter, Officer, Servant, Pilate, People

Narrator:
¹When Jesus had spoken these words, he went forth with his disciples across the Kidron Valley, where there was a garden, which he and his disciples entered. Now Judas, who betrayed

him, also knew the place; for Jesus often met there with his disciples. So Judas, procuring a band of soldiers and some officers from the chief priests and the Pharisees, went there with lanterns and torches and weapons. Then Jesus, knowing all that was to befall him, came forward and said to them,

Jesus:
Whom do you seek?

Narrator:
They answered him,

People:
Jesus of Nazareth.

Narrator:
Jesus said to them,

Jesus:
Here I am.

Narrator:
Judas, who betrayed Jesus was standing with them. When Jesus said to them, "Here I am," they drew back and fell to the ground. Again Jesus asked them,

Jesus:
Whom do you seek?

Narrator:
And they said,

People:
Jesus of Nazareth

Narrator:
Jesus answered,

Jesus:
I told you here I am; so, if you seek me, let these others go.

Narrator:
This was to fulfill the word which Jesus had spoken, "Of those whom you gave me I lost not one." Then Simon Peter, having a sword, drew it and struck the high priest's slave and cut off his right ear. The slave's name was Malchus. Jesus said to Peter,

Jesus:

Put your sword into its sheath; shall I not drink the cup which the Father has given me?

Narrator:

So the band of soldiers and their captain and the officers of the Judeans seized Jesus and bound him. First they led him to Annas, the father-in-law of Caiaphas, who was high priest that year. It was Caiaphas who had given counsel to the Judeans that it was expedient that one person should die for the people.

Simon Peter followed Jesus, and so did another disciple. Being known to the high priest, that disciple entered the court of the high priest along with Jesus, while Peter stood outside at the door. So the other disciple, who was known to the high priest, went out and spoke to the maid who kept the door, and brought Peter in. The maid who kept the door said to Peter,

Maid:

Are not you also one of this man's disciples?

Narrator:

He said,

Peter:

I am not.

Narrator:

Now the servants and officers had made a charcoal fire, because it was cold, and they were standing and warming themselves; Peter also was with them, standing and warming himself.

The high priest then questioned Jesus about his disciples and his teaching. Jesus answered the high priest,

Jesus:

I have spoken openly to the world; I have always taught in synagogues and in the temple, where all the Jewish people come together; I have said nothing secretly. Why do you ask me? Ask those who have heard me, what I said to them; they know what I said.

Narrator:

When he had said this, one of the officers standing by struck Jesus with his hand, saying,

Officer:
Is that how you answer the high priest?

Narrator:
Jesus answered the officer,

Jesus:
If I have spoken wrongly, bear witness to the wrong; but if I have spoken rightly, why do you strike me?

Narrator:
Annas then sent Jesus bound to Caiaphas the high priest. Now Simon Peter was standing and warming himself. They said to Peter,

People:
Are not you also one of his disciples?

Narrator:
He denied it and said,

Peter:
I am not.

Narrator:
One of the servants of the high priest, a relative of the man whose ear Peter had cut off, asked,

Servant:
Did I not see you in the garden with him?

Narrator:
Peter again denied it; and at once the cock crowed.

Then they led Jesus from the house of Caiaphas to the praetorium. It was early. They themselves did not enter the praetorium, so that they might not be defiled, but might eat the passover. So Pilate went out to them and said,

Pilate:
What accusation do you bring against this man?

Narrator:
They answered Pilate,

People:
If this man were not an evildoer, we would not have handed him over.

Narrator:
Pilate said to them,

Pilate:
Take him yourselves and judge him by your own law.

Narrator:
The Judeans said to him,

People:
It is not lawful for us to put anyone to death.

Narrator:
This was to fulfill the word which Jesus had spoken to show by what death he was to die.

Pilate entered the praetorium again and called Jesus, saying,

Pilate:
Are you the King of the Jewish people?

Narrator:
Jesus answered,

Jesus:
Do you say this of your own accord, or did others say it to you about me?

Narrator:
Pilate answered,

Pilate:
Am I a Jew? Your own nation and the chief priests have handed you over to me; what have you done?

Narrator:
Jesus answered,

Jesus:
My dominion is not of this world; if my dominion were of this world, my servants would fight, that I might not be handed over to the Judeans; but my dominion is not from the world.

Narrator:
Pilate said to him,

Pilate:
So you are a king?

Narrator:
Jesus answered,

Jesus:
You say that I am a king. For this I was born, and for this I have come into the world, to bear witness to the truth. Every one who is of the truth hears my voice.

Narrator:
Pilate said to Jesus,

Pilate:
What is truth?

Narrator:
Having said this, Pilate went out to the Judeans again, and told them,

Pilate:
I find no crime in him. But you have a custom that I should release one person for you at the Passover; will you have me release for you the King of the Jewish people?

Narrator:
They cried out again,

People:
Not this man, but Barabbas!

Narrator:
Now Barabbas was a robber.

[1]Then Pilate took Jesus and scourged him. And the soldiers plaited a crown of thorns, and put it on his head, and arrayed him in a purple robe; they came up to Jesus, saying,

People:
Hail, King of the Jews!

Narrator:
and struck him with their hands. Pilate went out again, and said to them,

Pilate:
See, I am bringing him out to you, that you may know that I find no crime in him.

Narrator:
So Jesus came out, wearing the crown of thorns and the purple robe. Pilate said to them,

Pilate:
Behold the man!

Narrator:
When the chief priests and the officers saw him, they cried out,

People:
Crucify him, crucify him!

Narrator:
Pilate said to them,

Pilate:
Take him yourselves and crucify him, for I find no crime in him.

Narrator:
The Judeans answered him,

People:
We have a law, and by that law he ought to die, because he has made himself the Son of God.

Narrator:
When Pilate heard these words, he was the more afraid; he entered the praetorium again and said to Jesus,

Pilate:
Where are you from?

Narrator:
But Jesus gave no answer. Pilate therefore said to him,

Pilate:
You will not speak to me? Do you know that I have power to release you, and power to crucify you?

Narrator:
Jesus answered him,

Jesus:
You would have no power over me unless it had been given you from above; therefore the one who delivered me to you has the greater sin.

Narrator:
Upon this Pilate sought to release him, but the Judeans cried out,

People:
If you release this man, you are not Caesar's friend; every one who makes himself a king sets himself against Caesar.

Narrator:
When Pilate heard these words, he brought Jesus out and sat down on the judgment seat at a place called The Pavement, and in Hebrew, Gabbatha. Now it was the day of Preparation of the Passover; it was about the sixth hour. He said to the Judeans,

Pilate:
Behold your king!

Narrator:
They cried out,

People:
Away with him, away with him, crucify him!

Narrator:
Pilate said to them,

Pilate:
Shall I crucify your king?

Narrator:
The chief priests answered,

People:
We have no king but Caesar.

Narrator:
Then he handed him over to them to be crucified.

So they took Jesus, and he went out, bearing his own cross, to the place called the place of a skull, which is called in Hebrew Golgotha. There they crucified Jesus, and with him two others, one on either side, and Jesus between them. Pilate also wrote a title and put it on the cross; it read, "Jesus of Nazareth, the King of the Jews." Many of the Judeans read this title, for the place where Jesus was crucified was near the city; and it was written in Hebrew, in Latin, and in Greek. The chief priests of the Jewish people then said to Pilate,

People:
Do not write, "The King of the Jews," but, "This man said, I am King of the Jews."

Narrator:
Pilate answered,

Pilate:
What I have written I have written.

Narrator:
When the soldiers had crucified Jesus they took his garments and made four parts, one for each soldier; also his tunic. But his tunic was without seam, woven from top to bottom; so they said to one another,

People:
Let us not tear it, but cast lots for it to see whose it shall be.

Narrator:
This was to fulfil the scripture,

"They parted my garments among them,
and for my clothing they cast lots."

So the soldiers did this. But standing by the cross of Jesus were his mother, and his mother's sister, Mary the wife of Clopas, and Mary Magdalene. When Jesus saw his mother, and the disciple whom he loved standing near, he said to his mother,

Jesus:
Woman, behold your son!

Narrator:
Then he said to the disciple,

Jesus:
Behold, your mother!

Narrator:
And from that hour the disciple took her to his own home. After this Jesus, knowing that all was now finished, said (to fulfill the scripture),

Jesus:
I thirst.

Narrator:
A bowl full of vinegar stood there; so they put a sponge full of vinegar on hyssop and held it to his mouth. Having received the vinegar, Jesus said,

Jesus:
It is finished;

Narrator:
and with bowed head gave over the spirit.

Since it was the day of Preparation, in order to prevent the bodies from remaining on the cross on the sabbath (for that sabbath was a high day), the Judeans asked Pilate that their legs might be broken, and that they might be taken away. So the soldiers came and broke the legs of the first, and of the other who had been crucified with him; but when they came to Jesus and saw that he was already dead, they did not break his legs. But one of the soldiers pierced his side with a spear, and at once there came out blood and water. One who saw it whose testimony is true, and who knows that he tells the truth—has borne witness that you also may believe. For these things took place that the scripture might be fulfilled, "Not a bone of him shall be broken." [37]And again another scripture says, "They shall look upon the one whom they have pierced."

[38]After this Joseph of Arimathea, who was a disciple of Jesus, but secretly, for fear of the Judeans, asked Pilate that he might take away the body of Jesus, and Pilate gave him leave. So Joseph came and took away Jesus' body. Nicodemus also, who had at first come to Jesus by night, came bringing a mixture of myrrh and aloes, about a hundred pounds' weight. They took the body of Jesus, and bound it in linen cloths with the spices, as is the burial custom of the Jews. Now in the place where Jesus was crucified there was a garden, and in the garden a new tomb where no one had ever been laid. [42]So because of the Jewish day of Preparation, as the tomb was close at hand, they laid Jesus there.

THE EASTER VIGIL

READING

Genesis 1:1–2:3

[1]In the beginning God created the heavens and the earth. The earth was without form and void, and darkness was upon the face of the deep; and the Spirit of God was moving over the face of the waters.

And God said, "Let there be light"; and there was light. And God saw that the light was good; and God separated the light from the darkness. God called the light Day, and the darkness God called Night. And there was evening and there was morning, one day.

And God said, "Let there be a firmament in the midst of the waters, and let it separate the waters from the waters." And God made the firmament and separated the waters which were under the firmament from the waters which were above the firmament. And it was so. And God called the firmament Heaven. And there was evening and there was morning, a second day.

And God said, "Let the waters under the heavens be gathered together into one place, and let the dry land appear." And it was so. God called the dry land Earth, and the waters that were gathered together God called Seas. And God saw that it was good. And God said, "Let the earth put forth vegetation, plants yielding seed, and fruit trees bearing fruit in which is their seed, each according to its kind, upon the earth." And it was so. The earth brought forth vegetation, plants yielding seed according to their own kinds, and trees bearing fruit in which is their seed, each according to its kind. And God saw that it was good. And there was evening and there was morning, a third day.

And God said, "Let there be lights in the firmament of the heavens to separate the day from the night; and let them be for signs and for seasons and for days and years, and let them be lights in the firmament of the heavens to give light upon the earth." And it was so. And God made the two great lights, the greater light to rule the day, and the lesser light to rule the night; God made the stars also. And God set them in the firmament of the heavens to give light upon the earth, to rule over the day and night, and to separate the light from the darkness. And God saw that it was good. And there was evening and there was morning, a fourth day.

And God said, "Let the waters bring forth swarms of living creatures, and let birds fly above the earth across the firmament of the heavens." So God created the great sea monsters and every living creature that moves, with which the waters swarm, according to their kinds, and every winged bird according to its kind. And God saw that it was good. And God blessed them, saying, "Be fruitful and multiply and fill the waters in the seas, and let birds multiply on the earth." And there was evening and there was morning, a fifth day.

And God said, "Let the earth bring forth living creatures according to their kinds: cattle and creeping things and beasts of the earth according to their kinds." And it was so. And God made the beasts of the earth according to their kinds and the cattle according to their kinds, and everything that creeps upon the ground according to its kind. And God saw that it was good.

Then God said, "Let us make humankind in our image, after our likeness; and let them have dominion over the fish of the sea, and over the birds of the air, and over the cattle, and over all the earth, and over every creeping thing that creeps upon the earth." So God created humankind in the divine image; in the image of God humankind was created; male and female God created them. And God blessed them, and God said to them, "Be fruitful and multiply, and fill the earth and subdue it; and have dominion over the fish of the sea and over the birds of the air and over every living thing that moves upon the earth." And God said, "Behold, I have given you every plant yielding seed which is upon the face of all the earth, and every tree with seed in its fruit; you shall have them for food.

And to every beast of the earth, and to every bird of the air, and to everything that creeps on the earth, everything that has the breath of life, I have given every green plant for food." And it was so. And God saw everything that had been made, and behold, it was very good. And there was evening and there was morning, a sixth day.

Thus the heavens and the earth were finished, and all the host of them. And on the seventh day God finished the work which had been done, and God rested on the seventh day from all the work which God had done. ³So God blessed the seventh day and hallowed it, because on it God rested from all the work which God had done in creation.

READING

Genesis 7:1–5, 11–18, 8:6–18, 9:8–13

¹The LORD said to Noah, "Go into the ark, you and all your household, for I have seen that you are righteous before me in this generation. Take with you seven pairs of all clean animals, the male and his mate; and a pair of the animals that are not clean, the male and his mate; and seven pairs of the birds of the air also, male and female, to keep their kind alive upon the face of all the earth. For in seven days I will send rain upon the earth forty days and forty nights; and every living thing that I have made I will blot out from the face of the ground." ⁵And Noah did all that the LORD had commanded him.

¹¹In the six hundredth year of Noah's life, in the second month, on the seventeenth day of the month, on that day all the fountains of the great deep burst forth, and the windows of the heavens were opened. And rain fell upon the earth forty days and forty nights. On the very same day Noah and his sons, Shem and Ham and Japheth, and Noah's wife and the three wives of his sons with them entered the ark, they and every beast according to its kind, and all the cattle according to their kinds, and every creeping thing that creeps on the earth according to its kind, and every bird according to its kind, every bird of every sort. They went into the ark with Noah, two and

two of all flesh in which there was the breath of life. And they that entered, male and female of all flesh, went in as God had commanded him; and the LORD shut him in.

The flood continued forty days upon the earth; and the waters increased, and bore up the ark, and it rose high above the earth. [18]The waters prevailed and increased greatly upon the earth; and the ark floated on the face of the waters.

[6]At the end of forty days Noah opened the window of the ark which he had made, and sent forth a raven; and it went to and fro until the waters were dried up from the earth. Then he sent forth a dove from him, to see if the waters had subsided from the face of the ground; but the dove found no place to set its foot, and it returned to him to the ark, for the waters were still on the face of the whole earth. So Noah put forth his hand and took the dove and brought it into the ark with him. He waited another seven days, and again he sent forth the dove out of the ark; and the dove came back to him in the evening, and lo, in its mouth a freshly plucked olive leaf; so Noah knew that the waters had subsided from the earth. Then he waited another seven days, and sent forth the dove; and it did not return to him any more.

In the six hundred and first year, in the first month, the first day of the month, the waters were dried from off the earth; and Noah removed the covering of the ark, and looked, and behold, the face of the ground was dry. In the second month, on the twenty-seventh day of the month, the earth was dry. Then God said to Noah, "Go forth from the ark, you and your wife, and your sons and your sons' wives with you. Bring forth with you every living thing that is with you of all flesh—birds and animals and every creeping thing that creeps on the earth—that they may breed abundantly on the earth, and be fruitful and multiply upon the earth." [18]So Noah went forth, and his sons and his wife and his sons' wives with him.

[8]Then God said to Noah and to his sons with him, "Behold, I establish my covenant with you and your descendants after you, and with every living creature that is with you, the birds, the cattle, and every beast of the earth with you, as many as

came out of the ark. I establish my covenant with you, that never again shall all flesh be cut off by the waters of a flood, and never again shall there be a flood to destroy the earth." And God said, "This is the sign of the covenant which I make between me and you and every living creature that is with you, for all future generations; ¹³I set my bow in the cloud, and it shall be a sign of the covenant between me and the earth."

READING

Genesis 22:1–18

¹After these things God tested Abraham, and said to him, "Abraham!" And he said, "Here am I." God said, "Take your son, your only son Isaac, whom you love, and go to the land of Moriah, and offer him there as a burnt offering upon one of the mountains of which I shall tell you." So Abraham rose early in the morning, saddled his donkey, and took two of his servants with him, and his son Isaac; and he cut the wood for the burnt offering, and arose and went to the place of which God had told him. On the third day Abraham lifted up his eyes and saw the place afar off. Then Abraham said to his servants, "Stay here with the donkey; I and the lad will go yonder and worship, and come again to you." And Abraham took the wood of the burnt offering, and laid it on Isaac his son; and he took in his hand the fire and the knife. So they went both of them together. And Isaac said to his father Abraham, "My father!" And he said, "Here am I, my son." He said, "Behold, the fire and the wood; but where is the lamb for a burnt offering?" Abraham said, "God will provide the lamb for a burnt offering to God, my son." So they went both of them together.

When they came to the place of which God had told him, Abraham built an altar there, and laid the wood in order, and bound Isaac his son, and laid him on the altar, upon the wood. Then Abraham put forth his hand, and took the knife to slay his son. But the angel of the LORD called to him from heaven, and said, "Abraham, Abraham!" And he said, "Here am I." The angel said, "Do not lay your hand on the lad or do anything to him; for now I know that you fear God, seeing you have not withheld your son, your only son, from me." And

Abraham lifted up his eyes and looked, and behold, behind him was a ram, caught in a thicket by its horns; and Abraham went and took the ram, and offered it up as a burnt offering instead of his son. So Abraham called the name of that place The LORD will provide; as it is said to this day, "On the mount of the LORD it shall be provided."

And the angel of the LORD called to Abraham a second time from heaven, and said, "By myself I have sworn, says the LORD, because you have done this, and have not withheld your son, your only son, I will indeed bless you, and I will multiply your descendants as the stars of heaven and as the sand which is on the seashore. And your descendants shall possess the gate of their enemies, [18]and by your descendants shall all the nations of the earth bless themselves, because you have obeyed my voice."

READING

Exodus 12:1–14

[1]The LORD said to Moses and Aaron in the land of Egypt, "This month shall be for you the beginning of months; it shall be the first month of the year for you. Tell all the congregation of Israel that on the tenth day of this month they shall take every man a lamb according to their fathers' houses, a lamb for a household; and if the household is too small for a lamb, then a man and his neighbor next to his house shall take according to the number of persons; according to what each can eat you shall make your count for the lamb. Your lamb shall be without blemish, a male a year old; you shall take it from the sheep or from the goats; and you shall keep it until the fourteenth day of this month, when the whole assembly of the congregation of Israel shall kill their lambs in the evening. Then they shall take some of the blood, and put it on the two doorposts and the lintel of the houses in which they eat them. They shall eat the flesh that night, roasted; with unleavened bread and bitter herbs they shall eat it. Do not eat any of it raw or boiled with water, but roasted, its head with its legs and its inner parts. And you shall let none of it remain until the morning, anything that remains until the morning you shall burn. In this manner

you shall eat it; your loins girded, your sandals on your feet, and your staff in your hand; and you shall eat it in haste. It is the LORD's passover. For I will pass through the land of Egypt that night, and I will smite all the first-born in the land of Egypt, both human and animal; and on all the gods of Egypt I will execute judgments: I am the LORD. The blood shall be a sign for you, upon the houses where you are; and when I see the blood, I will pass over you, and no plague shall fall upon you to destroy you, when I smite the land of Egypt.

¹⁴"This day shall be for you a memorial day, and you shall keep it as a feast to the LORD; throughout your generations you shall observe it as an ordinance for ever."

READING

Exodus 14:10–15:1

¹⁰When the Pharoah drew near, the people of Israel lifted up their eyes, and behold, the Egyptians were marching after them; and they were in great fear. And the people of Israel cried out to the LORD; and they said to Moses, "Is it because there are no graves in Egypt that you have taken us away to die in the wilderness? What have you done to us, bringing us out of Egypt? Is not this what we said to you in Egypt, 'Let us alone and let us serve the Egyptians'? For it would have been better for us to serve the Egyptians than to die in the wilderness." And Moses said to the people, "Fear not, stand firm, and see the salvation of the LORD, which the LORD will work for you today; for the Egyptians whom you see today, you shall never see again. The LORD will fight for you, and you have only to be still." The LORD said to Moses, "Why do you cry to me? Tell the people of Israel to go forward. Lift up your rod, and stretch out your hand over the sea and divide it, that the people of Israel may go on dry ground through the sea. And I will harden the hearts of the Egyptians so that they shall go in after them, and I will get glory over Pharoah and all his host, his chariots, and his horsemen. And the Egyptians shall know that I am the LORD, when I have gotten glory over Pharoah, his chariots, and his horsemen."

Then the angel of God who went before the host of Israel moved and went behind them; and the pillar of cloud moved from before them and stood behind them, coming between the host of Egypt and the host of Israel. And there was the cloud and the darkness; and the night passed without one coming near the other all night.

Then Moses stretched out his hand over the sea; and the LORD drove the sea back by a strong east wind all night, and made the sea dry land, and the waters were divided. And the people of Israel went into the midst of the sea on dry ground, the waters being a wall to them on their right hand and on their left. The Egyptians pursued, and went in after them into the midst of the sea, all Pharoah's horses, his chariots, and his horsemen. And in the morning watch the LORD in the pillar of fire and of cloud looked down upon the host of the Egyptians, and discomfited the host of the Egyptians, clogging their chariot wheels so that they drove heavily; and the Egyptians said, "Let us flee from before Israel; for the LORD fights for them against the Egyptians."

Then the LORD said to Moses, "Stretch out your hand over the sea, that the water may come back upon the Egyptians, upon their chariots, and upon their horsemen." So Moses stretched forth his hand over the sea, and the sea returned to its wonted flow when the morning appeared; and the Egyptians fled into it, and the LORD routed the Egyptians in the midst of the sea. The waters returned and covered the chariots and the horsemen and all the host of Pharoah that had followed them into the sea; not so much as one of them remained. But the people of Israel walked on dry ground through the sea, the waters being a wall to them on their right hand and on their left.

Thus the LORD saved Israel that day from the hand of the Egyptians; and Israel saw the Egyptians dead upon the seashore. And Israel saw the great work which the LORD did against the Egyptians, and the people feared the LORD; and they believed in the LORD and in Moses, the servant of the LORD.

¹Then Moses and the people of Israel sang this song to the LORD, saying,

"I will sing to the LORD who has triumphed gloriously;
the horse and its rider have been thrown into the sea."

READING

Isaiah 4:2–6

²In that day the branch of the LORD shall be beautiful and glorious, and the fruit of the land shall be the pride and glory of the survivors of Israel. And the one who is left in Zion and remains in Jerusalem will be called holy, every one who has been recorded for life in Jerusalem, when the Lord shall have washed away the filth of the people of Zion and cleansed the bloodstains of Jerusalem from its midst by a spirit of judgment and by a spirit of burning. Then the LORD will create over the whole site of Mount Zion and over its assemblies a cloud by day, and smoke and the shining of a flaming fire by night; for over all the glory there will be a canopy and a pavilion. ⁶It will be for a shade by day from the heat, and for a refuge and a shelter from the storm and rain.

READING

Isaiah 55:1–11

¹"Ho, every one who thirsts,
    come to the waters;
and whoever has no money,
    come, buy and eat!
Come, buy wine and milk
    without money and without price.
Why do you spend your money for that which is not bread,
    and your labor for that which does not satisfy?
Hearken diligently to me, and eat what is good,
    and delight yourselves in fatness.
Incline your ear, and come to me;
    hear, that your soul may live;

and I will make with you an everlasting covenant,
    my steadfast, sure love for David.
Behold, I made him a witness to the peoples,
    a leader and commander for the peoples.
Behold, you shall call nations that you know not,
    and nations that knew you not shall run to you,
because of the LORD your God, and of the Holy One of Israel,
    for the LORD has glorified you.
Seek the LORD while the LORD may be found,
    call upon God, while God is near;
let the wicked forsake their ways,
    and the unrighteous their thoughts;
let them return to the LORD, who will have mercy on them,
    and to our God, who will abundantly pardon.
For my thoughts are not your thoughts,
    neither are your ways my ways, says the LORD.
For as the heavens are higher than the earth,
    so are my ways higher than your ways
    and my thoughts than your thoughts.
For as the rain and the snow come down from heaven,
    and return not thither but water the earth,
making it bring forth and sprout,
    giving seed to the sower and bread to the eater,
[11]so shall my word be that goes forth from my mouth;
    it shall not return to me empty,
but it shall accomplish that which I purpose,
    and prosper in the thing for which I sent it."

READING

Ezekiel 37:1–14

[1]The hand of the LORD was upon me, and brought me out by
the Spirit of the LORD, and set me down in the midst of the
valley; it was full of bones. And the LORD led me round among
them; and behold, there were very many upon the valley; and
lo, they were dry. And the LORD said to me, "O human one,
can these bones live?" And I answered, "O Lord GOD, you
know." Again the LORD said to me, "Prophesy to these bones,

and say to them, O dry bones, hear the word of the LORD. Thus says the Lord GOD to these bones: Behold, I will cause breath to enter you, and you shall live. And I will lay sinews upon you, and will cause flesh to come upon you, and cover you with skin, and put breath in you, and you shall live; and you shall know that I am the LORD."

So I prophesied as I was commanded; and as I prophesied, there was a noise, and behold, a rattling; and the bones came together, bone to its bone. And as I looked, there were sinews on them, and flesh had come upon them, and skin had covered them; but there was no breath in them. Then the LORD said to me, "Prophesy to the breath, prophesy, O human one, and say to the breath, Thus says the Lord GOD: Come from the four winds, O breath, and breathe upon these slain, that they may live." So I prophesied as the LORD commanded me, and the breath came into them, and they lived, and stood upon their feet, an exceedingly great host.

Then the LORD said to me, "O human one, these bones are the whole house of Israel. Behold, they say, 'Our bones are dried up, and our hope is lost; we are clean cut off.' Therefore prophesy, and say to them, Thus says the Lord GOD: Behold, I will open your graves, and raise you from your graves, O my people; and I will bring you home into the land of Israel. And you shall know that I am the LORD, when I open your graves, and raise you from your graves, O my people. ¹⁴And I will put my Spirit within you, and you shall live, and I will place you in your own land; then you shall know that I, the LORD, have spoken, and I have done it, says the LORD."

R L   Baruch 3:9–4:4

⁹Hear the commandments of life, O Israel;
    give ear, and learn wisdom!
Why is it, O Israel, why is it that you are in the land of your
        enemies,
    that you are growing old in a foreign country,
that you are defiled with the dead,
    that you are counted among those in Hades?

You have forsaken the fountain of wisdom.
If you had walked in the way of God,
   you would be dwelling in peace for ever.
Learn where there is wisdom,
   where there is strength,
   where there is understanding,
that you may at the same time discern
   where there is length of days, and life,
   where there is light for the eyes, and peace.
Who has found the place of Wisdom?
   And who has entered her storehouses?
Where are the rulers of the nations,
   and those who govern the beasts on the earth,
those who have sport with the birds of the air,
   and who hoard up silver and gold,
in which people trust,
   and there is no end to their getting;
those who scheme to get silver, and are anxious,
   whose labors are beyond measure?
They have vanished and gone down to Hades,
   and others have arisen in their place.
Youths have seen the light of day,
   and have dwelt upon the earth;
but they have not learned the way to knowledge,
   nor understood her paths,
   nor laid hold of her.
Their children have stayed far from her way.
She has not been heard of in Canaan,
   nor seen in Teman;
the children of Hagar, who seek for understanding on the
      earth,
   the merchants of Merran and Teman,
   the story-tellers and the seekers for understanding,
have not learned the way to Wisdom,
   nor given thought to her paths.
O Israel, how great is the house of God!
   and how vast the territory that God possesses!
It is great and has no bounds;
   it is high and immeasurable.

The giants were born there, who were famous of old,
    great in stature, expert in war.
God did not choose them,
    nor give them the way to knowledge;
so they perished because they had no wisdom,
    they perished through their folly.
Who has gone up into heaven, and taken her,
    and brought her down from the clouds?
Who has gone over the sea, and found her,
    and will buy her for pure gold?
No one knows the way to her,
    or is concerned about the path to her.
But the one who knows all things knows her,
    and found her through understanding.
The one who prepared the earth for all time
    filled it with four-footed creatures;
the one who sends forth the light, and it goes,
    called it, and it hearkened in fear;
the stars shone in their watches, and were glad;
    God called them, and they said, "Here we are!"
    They shone with gladness for the one who made them.
This is our God,
    with whom none other can be compared.
God found the whole way to knowledge,
    and gave her to Jacob, God's servant,
    and to Israel, the one whom God loved.
Afterward she appeared upon earth
    and lived among humankind.
She is the book of the commandments of God,
    and the law that endures for ever.
All who hold her fast will live,
    and those who forsake her will die.
Turn, O Jacob, and take her;
    walk toward the shining of her light.
Do not give your glory to another,
    or your advantages to an alien people.
4Happy are we, O Israel,
    for we know what is pleasing to God.

READING

R   E   Romans 6:3–11

³Do you not know that all of us who have been baptized into Christ Jesus were baptized into his death? We were buried therefore with Christ by baptism into death, so that as Christ was raised from the dead by the glory of the Father, we too might walk in newness of life.

For if we have been united with Christ in a death like his, we shall certainly be united with him in a resurrection like his. We know that our old self was crucified with Christ so that the sinful body might be destroyed, and we might no longer be enslaved to sin. For the one who has died is freed from sin. But if we have died with Christ, we believe that we shall also live with him. For we know that Christ being raised from the dead will never die again; death no longer has dominion over him. The death he died he died to sin, once for all, but the life he lives he lives to God. ¹¹So you also must consider yourselves dead to sin and alive to God in Christ Jesus.

READING

L   Colossians 3:1–4

¹If then you have been raised with Christ, seek the things that are above, where Christ is, seated at the right hand of God. Set your minds on things that are above, not on things that are on earth. For you have died, and your life is hid with Christ in God. ⁴When Christ who is our life appears, then you also will appear with him in glory.

GOSPEL

R   E   L   Matthew 28:1–10

¹Now after the sabbath, toward the dawn of the first day of the week, Mary Magdalene and the other Mary went to see the sepulchre. And behold, there was a great earthquake; for an angel of the Lord descended from heaven and came and rolled back the stone, and sat upon it. The appearance of the angel was like lightning, and its raiment white as snow. And for fear

of the angel the guards trembled and became as if dead. But the angel said to the women. "Do not be afraid; for I know that you seek Jesus who was crucified. He is not here; for he has risen, as he said. Come, see the place where he lay. Then go quickly and tell his disciples that he has risen from the dead, and behold, he is going before you to Galilee; there you will see him. Lo, I have told you." So they departed quickly from the tomb with fear and great joy, and ran to tell his disciples. And behold, Jesus met them and said, "Hail!" And they came up and took hold of Jesus' feet and worshiped him. [10]Then Jesus said to them, "Do not be afraid; go and tell my brothers to go to Galilee, and there they will see me."

R E L EASTER DAY, THE RESURRECTION OF OUR LORD

FIRST READING

R   Acts 10:34a, 37–43

E L   Acts 10:34–43

[34a]Peter opened his mouth and said: [34b]"Truly I perceive that God shows no partiality, but in every nation any one who is God-fearing and does what is right is acceptable to God. You know the word which God sent to Israel, preaching good news of peace by Jesus Christ (who is Lord of all), [37]the word which was proclaimed throughout all Judea, beginning from Galilee after the baptism which John preached: how God anointed Jesus of Nazareth with the Holy Spirit and with power; how Jesus went about doing good and healing all that were oppressed by the devil, for God was with him. And we are witnesses to all that Jesus did both in the country of the Judeans and in Jerusalem. They put him to death by hanging him on a tree; but God raised Jesus on the third day and made him manifest; not to all the people but to us who were chosen by God as witnesses, who ate and drank with Jesus after he rose from the dead. And Jesus commanded us to preach to the people, and to testify that he is the one ordained by God to be judge of the living and the dead. [43]To this Jesus all the prophets bear witness that every one who believes in him receives forgiveness of sins through his name."

SECOND READING

R E L   Colossians 3:1–4

[1]If then you have been raised with Christ, seek the things that are above, where Christ is, seated at the right hand of God. Set your minds on things that are above, not on things that are on earth. For you have died, and your life is hid with Christ in God. [4]When Christ who is our life appears, then you also will appear with him in glory.

GOSPEL

R L   John 20:1–9

E   John 20:1–10

¹Now on the first day of the week Mary Magdalene came to the tomb early, while it was still dark, and saw that the stone had been taken away from the tomb. So she ran, and went to Simon Peter and the other disciple, the one whom Jesus loved, and said to them, "They have taken the Lord out of the tomb, and we do not know where they have laid him." Peter then came out with the other disciple, and they went toward the tomb. They both ran, but the other disciple outran Peter and reached the tomb first; and stooping to look in, he saw the linen cloths lying there, but did not go in. Then Simon Peter came, following him, and went into the tomb; he saw the linen cloths lying, and the napkin, which had been on Jesus' head, not lying with the linen cloths but rolled up in a place by itself. Then the other disciple, who reached the tomb first, also went in, and he saw and believed; ⁹for as yet they did not know the scripture, that Jesus must rise from the dead. ¹⁰Then the disciples went back to their homes.

ALTERNATE GOSPEL

E L   Matthew 28:1–10

¹Now after the sabbath, toward the dawn of the first day of the week, Mary Magdalene and the other Mary went to see the sepulchre. And behold, there was a great earthquake; for an angel of the Lord descended from heaven and came and rolled back the stone, and sat upon it. The appearance of the angel was like lightning, and its raiment white as snow. And for fear of the angel the guards trembled and became as if dead. But the angel said to the women, "Do not be afraid; for I know that you seek Jesus who was crucified. He is not here; for he has risen, as he said. Come, see the place where he lay. Then go quickly and tell his disciples that he has risen from the dead, and behold, he is going before you to Galilee; there you will see him. Lo, I have told you." So they departed quickly from the tomb with fear and great joy, and ran to tell his disciples.

And behold, Jesus met them and said, "Hail!" And they came up and took hold of Jesus' feet and worshiped him. [10]Then Jesus said to them, "Do not be afraid; go and tell my brothers to go to Galilee, and there they will see me."

FIRST READING

R   Acts 2:42–47

42They who were baptized devoted themselves to the apostles' teaching and common life, to the breaking of bread and the prayers.

And fear came upon every soul; and many wonders and signs were done through the apostles. And all who believed were together and had all things in common; and they sold their possessions and goods and distributed them to all, as any had need. And day by day, attending the temple together and breaking bread in their homes, they partook of food with glad and generous hearts, 47praising God and having favor with the people. And the Lord added to their number day by day those who were being saved.

E L   Acts 2:14a, 22–32

14aPeter, standing with the eleven, lifted up his voice and addressed them,

22"O Israelites, hear these words: Jesus of Nazareth, a man attested to you by God with mighty works and wonders and signs which God did through him in your midst, as you yourselves know—this Jesus, delivered up according to the definite plan and foreknowledge of God, you crucified and killed by the hands of the lawless. But God raised him up, having loosed the pangs of death, because it was not possible for Jesus to be held by it. For David says concerning him,

'I saw the Lord always before me,
who is at my right hand that I may not be shaken;
therefore my heart was glad, and my tongue rejoiced;
moreover my flesh will dwell in hope.
For you will not abandon my soul to Hades,
nor let your Holy One see corruption.
You have made known to me the ways of life;
you will make me full of gladness with your presence.'

"My dear people, I may say to you confidently of the patriarch David that he both died and was buried, and his tomb is with us to this day. Being therefore a prophet, and knowing that God had sworn with an oath to him that God would set one of his descendants upon his throne, he foresaw and spoke of the resurrection of the Christ, that he was not abandoned to Hades, nor did his flesh see corruption. ³²This Jesus God raised up, and of that we all are witnesses."

SECOND READING

R E L   1 Peter 1:3–9

³Blessed be the God and Father of our Lord Jesus Christ, by whose great mercy we have been born anew to a living hope through the resurrection of Jesus Christ from the dead, and to an inheritance which is imperishable, undefiled, and unfading, kept in heaven for you, who by God's power are guarded through faith for a salvation ready to be revealed in the last time. In this you rejoice, though now for a little while you may have to suffer various trials, so that the genuineness of your faith, more precious than gold which though perishable is tested by fire, may redound to praise and glory and honor at the revelation of Jesus Christ, whom without having seen you love; though you do not now see Jesus, you believe in him and rejoice with unutterable and exalted joy. ⁹As the outcome of your faith you obtain the salvation of your souls.

GOSPEL

R E L   John 20:19–31

¹⁹On the evening of that day, the first day of the week, the doors being shut where the disciples were, for fear of the Judeans, Jesus came and stood among them and said to them, "Peace be with you." Having said this, Jesus showed them his hands and his side. Then the disciples were glad when they saw the Lord. Jesus said to them again, "Peace be with you. As the Father has sent me, even so I send you." Having said this, Jesus breathed on them, and said to them, "Receive the Holy Spirit. If you forgive the sins of any, they are forgiven; if you retain the sins of any, they are retained."

Now Thomas, one of the twelve, called the Twin, was not with them when Jesus came. So the other disciples told Thomas, "We have seen the Lord." But he said to them, "Unless I see in his hands the print of the nails, and place my finger in the mark of the nails, and place my hand in his side, I will not believe."

Eight days later, Jesus' disciples were again in the house, and Thomas was with them. The doors were shut, but Jesus came and stood among them, and said, "Peace be with you." Then Jesus said to Thomas, "Put your finger here, and see my hands; and put out your hand, and place it in my side; do not be faithless, but believing." Thomas answered Jesus, "My Lord and my God!" Jesus said to him, "Have you believed because you have seen me? Blessed are those who have not seen and yet believe."

Now Jesus did many other signs in the presence of the disciples, which are not written in this book; [31]but these are written that you may believe that Jesus is the Christ, the Son of God, and that believing you may have life in his name.

THIRD SUNDAY OF EASTER

FIRST READING

R   Acts 2:14a, 22–33

[14a]Peter, standing with the eleven, lifted up his voice and addressed them,

[22]"O Israelites, hear these words: Jesus of Nazareth, a man attested to you by God with mighty works and wonders and signs which God did through him in your midst, as you yourselves know—this Jesus, delivered up according to the definite plan and foreknowledge of God, you crucified and killed by the hands of the lawless. But God raised him up, having loosed the pangs of death, because it was not possible for Jesus to be held by it. For David says concerning him,

'I saw the Lord always before me,
who is at my right hand that I may not be shaken;
therefore my heart was glad, and my tongue rejoiced;
moreover my flesh will dwell in hope.
For you will not abandon my soul to Hades,
nor let your Holy One see corruption.
You have made known to me the ways of life;
you will make me full of gladness with your presence.'

"My dear people, I may say to you confidently of the patriarch David that he both died and was buried, and his tomb is with us to this day. Being therefore a prophet, and knowing that God had sworn with an oath to him that God would set one of his descendants upon his throne, he foresaw and spoke of the resurrection of the Christ, that he was not abandoned to Hades, nor did his flesh see corruption. This Jesus God raised up, and of that we are all witnesses. [33]Being therefore exalted at the right hand of God, and having received from the Father the promise of the Holy Spirit, Jesus has poured out this which you see and hear."

E L   Acts 2:14a, 36–47

[14a]Peter, standing with the eleven, lifted up his voice and addressed them,

[36]"Let all the house of Israel therefore know assuredly that God has made this Jesus whom you crucified to be both Lord and Christ."

Now when they heard this they were cut to the heart, and said to Peter and the rest of the apostles, "Brothers, what shall we do?" And Peter said to them, "Repent, and be baptized every one of you in the name of Jesus Christ for the forgiveness of your sins; and you shall receive the gift of the Holy Spirit. For the promise is to you and to your children and to all that are far off, everyone whom the Lord our God invites." And Peter testified with many other words and exhorted them, saying, "Save youselves from this crooked generation." So those who received Peter's word were baptized, and there were added that day about three thousand souls.

They who were baptized devoted themselves to the apostles' teaching and common life, to the breaking of bread and the prayers.

And fear came upon every soul; and many wonders and signs were done through the apostles. And all who believed were together and had all things in common; and they sold their possessions and goods and distributed them to all, as any had need. And day by day, attending the temple together and breaking bread in their homes, they partook of food with glad and generous hearts, [47]praising God and having favor with all the people. And the Lord added to their number day by day those who were being saved.

SECOND READING

R L   1 Peter 1:17–21
  E   1 Peter 1:17–23

[17]If you invoke as Father the one who judges all people impartially according to their deeds, conduct yourselves with fear throughout the time of your exile. You know that you were ransomed from the futile ways inherited from your forebears, not with perishable things such as silver or gold, but with the precious blood of Christ, like that of a lamb without blemish or spot. Christ was destined before the foundation of the world

but was made manifest at the end of the times for your sake. [21]Through Christ you have confidence in God, who raised him from the dead and gave him glory, so that your faith and hope are in God.

[22]Having purified your souls by your obedience to the truth for a sincere love of the community, love one another earnestly from the heart. [23]You have been born anew, not of perishable seed but of imperishable, through the living and abiding word of God.

GOSPEL

R E L   Luke 24:13–35

[13]That very day two of the disciples were going to a village named Emmaus, about seven miles from Jerusalem, and talking with each other about all these things that had happened. While they were talking and discussing together, Jesus himself drew near and went with them. But their eyes were kept from recognizing him. And Jesus said to them, "What is this conversation which you are holding with each other as you walk?" And they stood still, looking sad. Then one of them, named Cleopas, answered him, "Are you the only visitor to Jerusalem who does not know the things that have happened there in these days?" And Jesus said to them, "What things?" And they said to him, "Concerning Jesus of Nazareth, who was a prophet mighty in deed and word before God and all the people, and how our chief priests and rulers delivered him up to be condemned to death, and crucified him. But we had hoped that Jesus was the one to redeem Israel. Yes, besides all this, it is now the third day since this happened. Moreover, some women of our company amazed us. They were at the tomb early this morning and did not find his body; and they came back saying that they had seen a vision of angels, who said that Jesus was alive. Some of those who were with us went to the tomb, and found it just as the women had said; but Jesus they did not see." And Jesus said to them, "O foolish ones, and slow of heart to believe all that the prophets have spoken! Was it not necessary that the Christ should suffer these things and enter into his glory?" And beginning with Moses

and all the prophets, Jesus interpreted to them in all the scriptures the things concerning himself.

So they drew near to the village to which they were going. Jesus appeared to be going further, but they constrained him, saying, "Stay with us, for it is toward evening and the day is now far spent." So he went in to stay with them. When Jesus was at table with them, he took the bread and blessed, and broke it, and gave it to them. And their eyes were opened and they recognized him; and he vanished out of their sight. They said to each other, "Did not our hearts burn within us while he talked to us on the road, while he opened to us the scriptures?" And they rose that same hour and returned to Jerusalem; and they found the eleven gathered together and those who were with them, who said, "The Lord has risen indeed, and has appeared to Simon!" 35Then they told what had happened on the road, and how Jesus was known to them in the breaking of the bread.

FIRST READING

R   Acts 2:14a, 36–41

[14a]Peter, standing with the eleven, lifted up his voice and addressed them,

[36]"Let all the house of Israel therefore know assuredly that God has made this Jesus whom you crucified to be both Lord and Christ."

Now when they heard this they were cut to the heart, and said to Peter and the rest of the apostles, "Brothers, what shall we do?" And Peter said to them, "Repent, and be baptized every one of you in the name of Jesus Christ for the forgiveness of your sins; and you shall receive the gift of the Holy Spirit. For the promise is to you and to your children and to all that are far off, everyone whom the Lord our God invites. And Peter testified with many other words and exhorted them, saying, "Save yourselves from this crooked generation." [41]So those who received Peter's word were baptized, and there were added that day about three thousand souls.

E L   Acts 6:1–9, 7:2a, 51–60

[1]Now in these days when the disciples were increasing in number, the Hellenists murmured against the Hebrews because their widows were neglected in the daily distribution. And the twelve summoned the body of the disciples and said, "It is not right that we should give up preaching the word of God to serve tables. Therefore, my dear people, pick out from among you seven men of good repute, full of the Spirit and of wisdom, whom we may appoint to this duty. But we will devote ourselves to prayer and to the ministry of the word." And what they said pleased the whole multitude, and they chose Stephen, who was full of faith and of the Holy Spirit, and Philip, and Prochorus, and Nicanor, and Timon, and Parmenas, and Nicolaus, a proselyte of Antioch. These they set before the apostles, and they prayed and laid their hands upon them.

And the word of God increased; and the number of the disciples multiplied greatly in Jerusalem, and a great many of the priests were obedient to the faith.

And Stephen, full of grace and power, did great wonders and signs among the people. [9]Then some of those who belonged to the synagogue of the Freed Slaves (as it was called), and of the Cyrenians, and of the Alexandrians, and of those from Cilicia and Asia, arose and disputed with Stephen.

[2a]And Stephen said,

[51]"You stiff-necked people, uncircumcised in heart and ears, you always resist the Holy Spirit. As your forebears did, so do you. Which of the prophets did not your forebears persecute? And they killed those who announced beforehand the coming of the Righteous One, whom you have now betrayed and murdered, you who received the law as delivered by angels and did not keep it."

Now when they heard these things they were enraged, and they ground their teeth against him. But Stephen, full of the Holy Spirit, gazed into heaven and saw the glory of God, and Jesus standing at the right hand of God; and he said, "Behold, I see the heavens opened, and the Man of Heaven standing at the right hand of God." But they cried out with a loud voice and stopped their ears and rushed together upon him. And they cast Stephen out of the city and stoned him; and the witnesses laid down their garments at the feet of a youth named Saul. And as they were stoning Stephen, he prayed, "Lord Jesus, receive my spirit." [60]And he knelt down and cried with a loud voice, "Lord, do not hold this sin against them." And when he had said this, he fell asleep.

SECOND READING

R   1 Peter 2:20–25
E L   1 Peter 2:19–25

[19]You are approved if, mindful of God, you endure pain while suffering unjustly. [20]For what credit is it, if when you do wrong and are beaten for it you take it patiently? But if when you do

right and suffer for it you take it patiently, you have God's approval. For to this you have been called, because Christ also suffered for you, leaving you an example, that you should follow in his steps. Christ committed no sin; no guile was found on his lips. When reviled, he did not revile in return; when suffering, he did not threaten; but he trusted to the one who judges justly. Christ himself bore our sins in his body on the tree, that we might die to sin and live to righteousness. By his wounds you have been healed. [25]For you were straying like sheep, but have now returned to the Shepherd and Guardian of your souls.

GOSPEL

R E L   John 10:1–10

[At that time Jesus said,]

[1]"Truly, truly, I say to you, whoever does not enter the sheepfold by the door but climbs in by another way is a thief and a robber; but the one who enters by the door is the shepherd of the sheep. To that one the gatekeeper opens; the sheep hear the voice of the shepherd who calls his own sheep by name and leads them out. Having brought out all his own, the shepherd goes before them, and the sheep follow the shepherd, for they know his voice. A stranger they will not follow, but they will run away, for they do not know the voice of strangers." This figure Jesus used with them, but they did not understand what he was saying to them.

So Jesus again said to them, "Truly, truly, I say to you, I am the door of the sheep. All who came before me are thieves and robbers; but the sheep did not heed them. I am the door; any one who enters by me will be saved, and will go in and out and find pasture. [10]The thief comes only to steal and kill and destroy; I came that they may have life, and have it abundantly."

FIRST READING

R   Acts 6:1–7

¹Now in these days when the disciples were increasing in number, the Hellenists murmured against the Hebrews because their widows were neglected in the daily distribution. And the twelve summoned the body of the disciples and said, "It is not right that we should give up preaching the word of God to serve tables. Therefore, my dear people, pick out from among you seven men of good repute, full of the Spirit and of wisdom, whom we may appoint to this duty. But we will devote ourselves to prayer and to the ministry of the word." And what they said pleased the whole multitude, and they chose Stephen, who was full of faith and of the Holy Spirit, and Philip, and Prochorus, and Nicanor, and Timon, and Parmenas, and Nicolaus, a proselyte of Antioch. These they set before the apostles, and they prayed and laid their hands upon them.

⁷And the word of God increased; and the number of disciples multiplied greatly in Jerusalem, and a great many of the priests were obedient to the faith.

E L   Acts 17:1–15

¹Now when Paul and Silas had passed through Amphipolis and Apollonia, they came to Thessalonica, where there was a synagogue of the Jewish people. And Paul went in, as was his custom, and for three weeks he argued with them from the scriptures, explaining and proving that it was necessary for the Christ to suffer and to rise from the dead, and saying, "This Jesus, whom I proclaim to you, is the Christ." And some of them were persuaded, and joined Paul and Silas; as did a great many of the devout Greeks and not a few of the leading women. But the Jewish people were jealous, and taking some wicked fellows of the rabble, they gathered a crowd, set the city in an uproar, and attacked the house of Jason, seeking to bring them out to the people. And when they could not find

them, they dragged Jason and some of the community before the city authorities, crying, "These people who have turned the world upside down have come here also, and Jason has received them; and they are all acting against the decrees of Caesar, saying that there is another king, Jesus." And the people and the city authorities were disturbed when they heard this. And when they had taken security from Jason and the rest, they let them go.

The community immediately sent Paul and Silas away by night to Beroea; and when they arrived they went into the synagogue of the Jewish people. Now these were more noble than those in Thessalonica, for they received the word with all eagerness, examining the scriptures daily to see if these things were so. Many of them therefore believed, with not a few Greek women of high standing as well as men. But when the Jewish people of Thessalonica learned that the word of God was proclaimed by Paul at Beroea also, they came there too, stirring up and inciting the crowds. Then the community immediately sent Paul off on his way to the sea, but Silas and Timothy remained there. [15]Those who conducted Paul brought him as far as Athens; and receiving a command for Silas and Timothy to come to him as soon as possible, they departed.

SECOND READING

R   1 Peter 2:4–9
E   1 Peter 2:1–10
L   1 Peter 2:4–10

[1]Put away all malice and all guile and insincerity and envy and all slander. Like newborn infants, long for the pure spiritual milk, that by it you may grow up to salvation; for you have tasted the kindness of the Lord.

[4]Come to the Lord, to that living stone, rejected by human beings but in God's sight chosen and precious; and like living stones be yourselves built into a spiritual house, to be a holy priesthood, to offer spiritual sacrifices acceptable to God through Jesus Christ. For it stands in scripture:

"Behold, I am laying in Zion a stone, a cornerstone chosen and
   precious,
   and the one who believes in it will not be put to shame."

To you therefore who believe, the stone is precious, but for
those who do not believe,

"The very stone which the builders rejected
has become the head of the corner,"

and

"A stone of offense, and
a rock of stumbling";

for they stumble because they disobey the word, as they were
destined to do.

⁹But you are a chosen race, a royal priesthood, a holy nation,
God's own people, that you may declare the wonderful deeds
of God who called you out of darkness into marvelous light.
¹⁰Once you were no people but now you are God's people;
once you had not received mercy but now you have received
mercy.

GOSPEL

R L   John 14:1–12
   E   John 14:1–14

[At that time Jesus said,]

¹"Let not your hearts be troubled; believe in God, believe also
in me. In my Father's house are many rooms; if it were not so,
would I have told you that I go to prepare a place for you? And
when I go and prepare a place for you, I will come again and
will take you to myself, that where I am you may be also. And
you know the way where I am going." Thomas said to Jesus,
"Lord, we do not know where you are going; how can we
know the way?" Jesus said to him, "I am the way, and the
truth, and the life; no one comes to the Father, but by me. If
you had known me, you would have known my Father also;
henceforth you know and have seen my Father."

Philip said to him, "Lord, show us the Father, and we shall be satisfied." Jesus said to him, "Have I been with you so long, and yet you do not know me, Philip? They who have seen me have seen the Father; how can you say, 'Show us the Father'? Do you not believe that I am in the Father and the Father in me? The words that I say to you I do not speak on my own authority; but the Father who dwells in me is the one who acts. Believe me that I am in the Father and the Father in me; or else believe me for the sake of the acts themselves.

[12]"Truly, truly, I say to you, they who believe in me will also do the acts that I do; and greater acts than these will they do, because I go to the Father. [13]Whatever you ask in my name, I will do it, that the Father may be glorified in the Son; [14]if you ask anything in my name, I will do it."

FIRST READING

R   Acts 8:5–8, 14–17

[5]Philip went down to a city of Samaria, and proclaimed to them the Christ. And the multitudes with one accord gave heed to what was said by Philip, when they heard him and saw the signs which he did. For unclean spirits came out of many who were possessed, crying with a loud voice; and many who were paralyzed or lame were healed. [8]So there was much joy in that city.

[14]Now when the apostles at Jerusalem heard that Samaria had received the word of God, they sent to them Peter and John, who came down and prayed for them that they might receive the Holy Spirit; for it had not yet fallen on any of them, but they had only been baptized in the name of the Lord Jesus. [17]Then Peter and John laid their hands on them and they received the Holy Spirit.

E L   Acts 17:22–31

[22]Paul, standing in the middle of the Areopagus, said: "O Athenians, I perceive that in every way you are very religious. For as I passed along, and observed the objects of your worship, I found also an altar with this inscription, 'To an unknown god.' What therefore you worship as unknown, this I proclaim to you. The God who made the world and everything in it, being Lord of heaven and earth, does not live in shrines made by human hands, nor is God served by human hands, as though needing anything, since that very God gives to all human beings life and breath and everything. And God made from one every nation of humankind to live on all the face of the earth, having determined allotted periods and the boundaries of their habitation, that they should seek God, in the hope that they might grope towards and find God. Yet God is not far from each one of us, for

'In God we live and move and have our being';

as even some of your poets have said,

'For we are indeed the offspring of God.'

Being then God's offspring, we ought not to think that the Deity is like gold, or silver, or stone, a representation by human art and imagination. Having overlooked the times of ignorance, God now commands all people everywhere to repent, [31]because God has fixed a day on which to judge the world in righteousness by a man whom God has appointed, and of this God has given assurance to all people by raising this one from the dead."

SECOND READING

R   1 Peter 3:15–18
E   1 Peter 3:8–18
L   1 Peter 3:15–22

[8]Finally, all of you, have unity of spirit, sympathy, love of the community, a tender heart and a humble mind. Do not return evil for evil or reviling for reviling; but on the contrary bless, for to this you have been called, that you may obtain a blessing. For

"They who would love life
and see good days,
let them keep their tongues from evil
and their lips from speaking guile;
let them turn away from evil and do right;
let them seek peace and pursue it.
For the eyes of the Lord are upon the righteous,
and the ears of the Lord are open to their prayer.
But the face of the Lord is against those that do evil."

Now who is there to harm you if you are zealous for what is right? But even if you do suffer for righteousness' sake, you will be blessed. Have no fear of them, nor be troubled, [15]but in your hearts reverence Christ as Lord. Always be prepared to make a defense to any one who calls you to account for the hope that is in you, yet do it with gentleness and reverence; and keep your conscience clear, so that, when you are abused, those who revile your good behavior in Christ may be put to shame. For it is better to suffer for doing right, if that should be God's will, than for doing wrong. [18]For Christ also died for sins once for all, the righteous for the unrighteous, that he might bring us to God, being put to death in the flesh but made alive in the spirit; [19]in which he went and preached to the spirits in prison, who formerly did not obey, when God's patience waited in the days of Noah, during the building of the ark, in which a few, that is, eight persons, were saved through water. Baptism, which corresponds to this, now saves you, not as a removal of dirt from the body but as an appeal to God for a clear conscience, through the resurrection of Jesus Christ, [22]who has gone into heaven and is at the right hand of God, with angels, authorities, and powers subject to him.

GOSPEL

R L   John 14:15–21

[At that time Jesus said,]

[15]"If you love me, you will keep my commandments. And I will pray the Father who will give you another Counselor, to be with you for ever, even the Spirit of truth, whom the world cannot receive, because it neither sees nor knows that Spirit; you know that Spirit, for that Spirit dwells in you, and will be in you.

"I will not leave you desolate; I will come to you. Yet a little while, and the world will see me no more, but you will see me; because I live, you will live also. In that day you will know that I am in my Father, and you in me, and I in you. [21]They who have my commandments and keep them are those who love me; and those who love me will be loved by my Father, and I will love them and manifest myself to them."

E   John 15:1–8

[At that time Jesus said,]

[1]"I am the true vine, and my Father is the vinedresser. Every branch of mine that bears no fruit, my Father takes away, and every branch that does bear fruit my Father prunes, that it may bear more fruit. You are already made clean by the word which I have spoken to you. Abide in me, and I in you. As the branch cannot bear fruit by itself, unless it abides in the vine,

neither can you, unless you abide in me. I am the vine, you are the branches. They who abide in me, and I in them, it is they that bear much fruit, for apart from me you can do nothing. Those who do not abide in me are cast forth as branches and wither; and the branches are gathered, thrown into the fire and burned. If you abide in me, and my words abide in you, ask whatever you will, and it shall be done for you. [8]By this my Father is glorified, that you bear much fruit and so prove to be my disciples."

FIRST READING

R E L Acts 1:1–11

¹In the first book, O Theophilus, I have dealt with all that Jesus began to do and teach, until the day when he was taken up, having given commandment through the Holy Spirit to the apostles whom he had chosen. To them Jesus presented himself alive after his passion by many proofs, appearing to them during forty days, and speaking of the dominion of God. And while staying with them Jesus charged them not to depart from Jerusalem, but to wait for the promise of the Father, which, he said, "you heard from me, for John baptized with water, but before many days you shall be baptized with the Holy Spirit."

So when they had come together, they asked Jesus, "Lord, will you at this time restore dominion to Israel?" Jesus said to them, "It is not for you to know times or seasons which the Father has fixed by divine authority. But you shall receive power when the Holy Spirit has come upon you; and you shall be my witnesses in Jerusalem and in all Judea and Samaria and to the end of the earth." And when he had said this, as they were looking on, Jesus was lifted up, and a cloud took him out of their sight. And while they were gazing into heaven as he went, behold, two men stood by them in white robes, ¹¹and said, "O Galileans, why do you stand looking into heaven? This Jesus, who was taken up from you into heaven, will come in the same way as you saw him go into heaven."

SECOND READING

R Ephesians 1:17–23
E Ephesians 1:15–23
L Ephesians 1:16–23

¹⁵Because I have heard of your faith in the Lord Jesus and your love toward all the saints, ¹⁶I do not cease to give thanks for you, remembering you in my prayers, ¹⁷that the God of our Lord Jesus Christ, the Father of glory, may give you a spirit of wisdom and of revelation, that you may know God, having the

eyes of your hearts enlightened, that you may know what is
the hope to which God has called you, what are the riches of
God's glorious inheritance in the saints, and what is the immeasurable greatness of God's power in us who believe, according to the working of God's great might which was acom-
plished in Christ when God raised Christ from the dead and
made him sit at the right hand of power in the heavenly places,
far above all rule and authority and power and dominion, and
above every name that is named, not only in this age but also
in that which is to come; and God has put all things under the
feet of Christ and has made him the head over all things for
the church, ²³which is the body of Christ, the fullness of the
one who fills all in all.

GOSPEL

R Matthew 28:16–20

¹⁶Now the eleven disciples went to Galilee, to the mountain to
which Jesus had directed them. And when they saw Jesus they
worshiped him; but some doubted. And Jesus came and said to
them, "All authority in heaven and on earth has been given to
me. Go therefore and make disciples of all nations, baptizing
them in the name of the Father and of the Son and of the Holy
Spirit, ²⁰teaching them to observe all that I have commanded
you; and lo, I am with you always, to the close of the age."

E Luke 24:49–53
L Luke 24:44–53

⁴⁴Jesus said to the disciples, "These are my words which I
spoke to you, while I was still with you, that everything written about me in the law of Moses and the prophets and the
psalms must be fulfilled." Then Jesus opened their minds to
understand the scriptures, and said to them, "Thus it is written, that the Christ should suffer and on the third day rise
from the dead, and that repentance and forgiveness of sins
should be preached in the name of Christ to all nations, beginning from Jerusalem. You are witnesses of these things. ⁴⁹And
behold, I send the promise of my Father upon you; but stay in
the city, until you are clothed with power from on high."

Then Jesus led them out as far as Bethany, and lifting up his hands he blessed them. While blessing them, he parted from them, and was carried up into heaven. And they returned to Jerusalem with great joy, [53]and were continually in the temple blessing God.

FIRST READING

R   Acts 1:12–14
E L   Acts 1:8–14

[At that time Jesus said,]

[8]"You shall receive power when the Holy Spirit has come upon you; and you shall be my witnesses in Jerusalem and in all Judea and Samaria and to the end of the earth." And when he had said this, as the disciples were looking on, Jesus was lifted up, and a cloud took him out of their sight. And while they were gazing into heaven as he went, behold, two men stood by them in white robes, and said, "O Galileans, why do you stand looking into heaven? This Jesus, who was taken up from you into heaven, will come in the same way as you saw him go into heaven."

[12]Then they returned to Jerusalem from the mount called Olivet, which is near Jerusalem, a sabbath day's journey away; and when they had entered, they went up to the upper room, where they were staying, Peter and John and James and Andrew, Philip and Thomas, Bartholomew and Matthew, James the son of Alphaeus and Simon the Zealot and Judas the son of James. [14]All these with one accord devoted themselves to prayer, together with the women and Mary the mother of Jesus, and with his brothers.

SECOND READING

R   1 Peter 4:13–16
E   1 Peter 4:12–19
L   1 Peter 4:12–17, 5:6–11

[12]Beloved, do not be surprised at the fiery ordeal which comes upon you to prove you, as though something strange were happening to you. [13]But rejoice in so far as you share Christ's sufferings, that you may also rejoice and be glad when his glory is revealed. If you are reproached for the name of Christ, you are blessed, because the spirit of glory and of God rests upon you. But let none of you suffer as a murderer, or a thief,

or a wrongdoer, or a mischief-maker; [16]yet if you suffer as a Christian, do not be ashamed, but under that name glorify God. [17]For the time has come for judgement to begin with the household of God; and if it begins with us, what will be the end of those who do not obey the gospel of God? [18]And

"If the righteous are scarcely saved,
where will the impious and sinner appear?"

[19]Therefore let those who suffer according to God's will do right and entrust their souls to a faithful Creator.

[6]Humble yourselves therefore under the mighty hand of God, that in due time God may exalt you. Cast all your anxieties on God, for God cares about you. Be sober, be watchful. Your adversary the devil prowls around like a roaring lion, seeking some one to devour. Resist the devil, firm in your faith, knowing that the same experience of suffering is required of your community throughout the world. And after you have suffered a little while, that very God of all grace, who has called you into eternal glory in Christ, will restore, establish, and strengthen you. [11]To God be the dominion for ever and ever. Amen.

GOSPEL

R   John 17:1–11a
E L   John 17:1–11

[1]When Jesus had spoken these words, he lifted up his eyes to heaven and said, "Father, the hour has come; glorify your Son that the Son may glorify you, since you have given him power over all flesh, to give eternal life to all whom you have given him. And this is eternal life, that they know you the only true God, and Jesus Christ whom you have sent. I glorified you on earth, having accomplished the work which you gave me to do; and now, Father, glorify me in your own presence with the glory which I had with you before the world was made.

"I have manifested your name to those whom you gave me out of the world; yours they were, and you gave them to me, and they have kept your word. Now they know that everything that you have given me is from you; for I have given them the words which you gave me, and they have received them and know in truth that I came from you; and they have believed that you sent me. I am praying for them; I am not praying for the world but for those whom you have given me, for they are yours; all mine are yours, and yours are mine, and I am glorified in them. [11a]And now I am no more in the world, but they are in the world, and I am coming to you. [11b]Holy Father, keep them in your name, which you have given me, that they may be one, even as we are one."

R PENTECOST SUNDAY
E L DAY OF PENTECOST

FIRST READING

R E Acts 2:1-11

¹When the day of Pentecost had come, the company were all together in one place. And suddenly a sound came from heaven like the rush of a mighty wind, and it filled all the house where they were sitting. And there appeared to them tongues as of fire, distributed and resting on each one of them. And they were all filled with the Holy Spirit and began to speak in other tongues, as the Spirit gave them utterance.

Now there were dwelling in Jerusalem Jewish people, devout people from every nation under heaven. And at this sound the multitude came together, and they were bewildered, because all heard them speaking in their own language. And they were amazed and wondered, saying, "Are not all these who are speaking Galileans? And how is it that we hear, all of us in our own native language? Parthians and Medes and Elamites and residents of Mesopotamia, Judea, and Cappadocia, Pontus and Asia, Phrygia and Pamphylia, Egypt and the parts of Libya belonging to Cyrene, and visitors from Rome, both Jewish born and proselytes, ¹¹Cretans and Arabians, we hear them telling in our own tongues the mighty works of God."

L Joel 2:28–29

²⁸"And it shall come to pass afterward,
   that I will pour out my spirit on all flesh;
your sons and your daughters shall prophesy,
   your elders shall dream dreams,
   and your youths shall see visions.
²⁹Even upon the menservants and maidservants
   in those days, I will pour out my spirit."

SECOND READING

R   1 Corinthians 12:3b–7, 12–13

E   1 Corinthians 12:4–13

[3b]No one speaking by the Spirit of God ever says "Jesus be cursed!" and no one can say "Jesus is Lord" except by the Holy Spirit.

[4]Now there are varieties of gifts, but the same Spirit; and there are varieties of service, but the same Lord; and there are varieties of working, but it is the same God who inspires them all in every one. [7]To each is given the manifestation of the Spirit for the common good. [8]To one is given through the Spirit the utterance of wisdom, and to another the utterance of knowledge according to the same Spirit, to another faith by the same Spirit, to another gifts of healing by the same Spirit, to another the working of miracles, to another prophesy, to another the ability to distinguish between spirits, to another various kinds of tongues, to another the interpretation of tongues. All these are inspired by one and the same Spirit, who chooses what to apportion to each one individually.

[12]For just as the body is one and has many parts, and all the parts of the body, though many, are one body, so it is with Christ. [13]For by one Spirit we were all baptized into one body— Jews or Greeks, slaves or free—and all were made to drink of one Spirit.

L   Acts 2:1–21

[1]When the day of Pentecost had come, the company were all together in one place. And suddenly a sound came from heaven like the rush of a mighty wind, and it filled all the house where they were sitting. And there appeared to them tongues as of fire, distributed and resting on each one of them. And they were all filled with the Holy Spirit and began to speak in other tongues, as the Spirit gave them utterance.

Now there were dwelling in Jerusalem Jewish people, devout people from every nation under heaven. And at this sound the multitude came together, and they were bewildered, because all heard them speaking in their own language. And they were amazed and wondered, saying, "Are not all these who are speaking Galileans? And how is it that we hear, all of us in our own native language? Parthians and Medes and Elamites and residents of Mesopotamia, Judea and Cappadocia, Pontus and Asia, Phrygia and Pamphylia, Egypt and the parts of Libya belonging to Cyrene, and visitors from Rome, both Jewish born and proselytes, Cretans and Arabians, we hear them telling in our own tongues the mighty works of God." And all were amazed and perplexed, saying to one another, "What does this mean?" But others mocking said, "They are filled with new wine."

But Peter, standing with the eleven, lifted up his voice and addressed them, "O you Jewish people and all who dwell in Jerusalem, let this be known to you, and give ear to my words. For these people are not drunk, as you suppose, since it is only the third hour of the day; but this is what was spoken by the prophet Joel:

'And in the last days it shall be, God declares,
that I will pour out my Spirit upon all flesh,
and your sons and your daughters shall prophesy,
and your youths shall see visions,
and your elders shall dream dreams;
yes, and on my menservants and my maidservants in those
    days
I will pour out my Spirit; and they shall prophesy.
And I will show wonders in the heaven above
and signs on the earth beneath,
blood, and fire, and vapor of smoke;
the sun shall be turned into darkness
and the moon into blood,
before the day of the Lord comes,
and great and manifest day.
21And it shall be that whoever calls on the name of the Lord
    shall be saved.'"

GOSPEL

John 20:19–23

¹⁹On the evening of that day, the first day of the week, the doors being shut where the disciples were, for fear of the Judeans, Jesus came and stood among them and said to them, "Peace be with you." Having said this, Jesus showed them his hands and his side. Then the disciples were glad when they saw the Lord. Jesus said to them again, "Peace be with you. As the Father has sent me, even so I send you." Having said this, Jesus breathed on them, and said to them, "Receive the Holy Spirit. ²³If you forgive the sins of any, they are forgiven; if you retain the sins of any, they are retained."

FIRST READING

R   Exodus 34:4b–6, 8–9

[4b]Moses rose early in the morning and went up on Mount Sinai, as the Lord had commanded him, and took in his hand
two tables of stone. And the Lord descended in the cloud and
stood with him there, and proclaimed the name of the Lord.
[6]The Lord passed before Moses, and proclaimed, "The Lord,
the Lord, a God merciful and gracious, slow to anger, and
abounding in steadfast love and faithfulness." [8]And Moses
made haste to bow his head toward the earth, and worshiped.
[9]And he said, "If now I have found favor in your sight, O
Lord, I pray you, let the Lord go in the midst of us, although it
is a stiff-necked people; and pardon our iniquity and our sin,
and take us for your inheritance."

E L   Genesis 1:1–2:3

[1]In the beginning God created the heavens and the earth. The
earth was without form and void, and darkness was upon the
face of the deep; and the Spirit of God was moving over the
face of the waters.

And God said, "Let there be light"; and there was light. And
God saw that the light was good; and God separated the light
from the darkness. God called the light Day, and the darkness
God called Night. And there was evening and there was morning, one day.

And God said, "Let there be a firmament in the midst of the
waters, and let it separate the waters from the waters." And
God made the firmament and separated the waters which were
under the firmament from the waters which were above the
firmament. And it was so. And God called the firmament
Heaven. And there was evening and there was morning, a second day.

And God said, "Let the waters under the heavens be gathered
together into one place, and let the dry land appear." And it
was so. God called the dry land Earth, and the waters that

were gathered together God called Seas. And God saw that it was good. And God said, "Let the earth put forth vegetation, plants yielding seed, and fruit trees bearing fruit in which is their seed, each according to its kind, upon the earth." And it was so. The earth brought forth vegetation, plants yielding seed according to their own kinds, and trees bearing fruit in which is their seed, each according to its kind. And God saw that it was good. And there was evening and there was morning, a third day.

And God said, "Let there be lights in the firmament of the heavens to separate the day from the night; and let them be for signs and for seasons and for days and years, and let them be lights in the firmament of the heavens to give light upon the earth." And it was so. And God made the two great lights, the greater light to rule the day, and the lesser light to rule the night; God made the stars also. And God set them in the firmament of the heavens to give light upon the earth, to rule over the day and over the night, and to separate the light from the darkness. And God saw that it was good. And there was evening and there was morning, a fourth day.

And God said, "Let the waters bring forth swarms of living creatures, and let birds fly above the earth across the firmament of the heavens." So God created the great sea monsters and every living creature that moves, with which the waters swarm, according to their kinds, and every winged bird according to its kind. And God saw that it was good. And God blessed them, saying, "Be fruitful and multiply and fill the waters in the seas, and let birds multiply on the earth." And there was evening and there was morning, a fifth day.

And God said, "Let the earth bring forth living creatures according to their kinds: cattle and creeping things and beasts of the earth according to their kinds." And it was so. And God made the beasts of the earth according to their kinds and the cattle according to their kinds, and everything that creeps upon the ground according to its kind. And God saw that it was good.

Then God said, "Let us make humankind in our image, after our likeness; and let them have dominion over the fish of the sea, and over the birds of the air, and over the cattle, and over all the earth, and over every creeping thing that creeps upon the earth." So God created humankind in the divine image; in the image of God humankind was created; male and female God created them. And God blessed them, and God said to them, "Be fruitful and multiply, and fill the earth and subdue it; and have dominion over the fish of the sea and over the birds of the air and over every living thing that moves upon the earth." And God said, "Behold, I have given you every plant yielding seed which is upon the face of all the earth, and every tree with seed in its fruit; you shall have them for food. And to every beast of the earth, and to every bird of the air, and to everything that creeps on the earth, everything that has the breath of life, I have given every green plant for food." And it was so. And God saw everything that had been made, and behold, it was very good. And there was evening and there was morning, a sixth day.

Thus the heavens and the earth were finished, and all the host of them. And on the seventh day God finished the work which had been done, and God rested on the seventh day from all the work which God had done. ³So God blessed the seventh day and hallowed it, because on it God rested from all the work which God had done in creation.

SECOND READING

R   2 Corinthians 13:11–13
E L   2 Corinthians 13:11–14

¹¹Finally, my dear people, farewell. Mend your ways, heed my appeal, agree with one another, live in peace, and the God of love and peace will be with you. Greet one another with a holy kiss. ¹³All the saints greet you.

¹⁴The grace of the Lord Jesus Christ and the love of God and the communion of the Holy Spirit be with you all.

GOSPEL

R   John 3:16–18

¹⁶For God loved the world in this way, that God gave the Son, the only begotten one, that whoever believes in him should not perish but have eternal life. For God sent the Son into the world, not to condemn the world, but that through the Son the world might be saved. ¹⁸Those who believe in him are not condemned; those who do not believe are condemned already, because they have not believed in the name of the only Son of God.

E L   Matthew 28:16–20

¹⁶Now the eleven disciples went to Galilee, to the mountain to which Jesus had directed them. And when they saw Jesus they worshiped him; but some doubted. And Jesus came and said to them, "All authority in heaven and on earth has been given to me. Go therefore and make disciples of all nations, baptizing them in the name of the Father and of the Son and of the Holy Spirit, ²⁰teaching them to observe all that I have commanded you; and lo, I am with you always, to the close of the age."

R CORPUS CHRISTI

FIRST READING

R Deuteronomy 8:2–3, 14–16

²"You shall remember all the way which the LORD your God has led you these forty years in the wilderness, that the LORD might humble you, testing you to know what was in your heart, whether you would keep God's commandments, or not. ³And the LORD humbled you and let you hunger and fed you with manna, which you did not know, nor did your forebears know; that the LORD might make you know that not by bread alone does one live, but by everything that proceeds out of the mouth of the LORD.

"¹⁴[Take heed, lest] you forget the LORD your God, who brought you out of the land of Egypt, out of the house of bondage, who led you through the great and terrible wilderness, with its fiery serpents and scorpions and thirsty ground where there was no water, who brought you water out of the flinty rock, ¹⁶who fed you in the wilderness with manna which your forebears did not know."

SECOND READING

R 1 Corinthians 10:16–17

¹⁶The cup of blessing which we bless, is it not a participation in the blood of Christ? The bread which we break, is it not a participation in the body of Christ? ¹⁷Because there is one bread, we who are many are one body, for we all partake of the one bread.

GOSPEL

R John 6:51–58

[At that time Jesus said:]

⁵¹"I am the living bread which came down from heaven; any who eat of this bread will live for ever; and the bread which I shall give for the life of the world is my flesh."

The Jewish people then disputed among themselves, saying, "How can this man give us his flesh to eat?" So Jesus to them, "Truly, truly, I say to you, unless you eat the flesh of the Man of Heaven and drink his blood, you have no life in you; they who eat my flesh and drink my blood have eternal life, and I will raise them up at the last day. For my flesh is food indeed, and my blood is drink indeed. They who eat my flesh and drink my blood abide in me, and I in them. As the living Father sent me, and I live because of the Father, so they who eat me will live because of me. [58]This is the bread which came down from heaven, not such as the forebears ate and died; they who eat this bread will live for ever."

R NINTH SUNDAY IN ORDINARY TIME
E PROPER 4
L SECOND SUNDAY AFTER PENTECOST

FIRST READING

R   Deuteronomy 11:18, 26–28, 32
E L Deuteronomy 11:18–21, 26–28

¹⁸"You shall therefore lay up these words of mine in your heart
and in your soul; and you shall bind them as a sign upon your
hand, and they shall be as frontlets between your eyes. ¹⁹And
you shall teach them to your children, talking of them when
you are sitting in your house, and when you are walking by
the way, and when you lie down, and when you rise. And you
shall write them upon the doorposts of your house and upon
your gates, ²¹that your days and the days of your children may
be multiplied in the land which the LORD swore to your forebears to give them, as long as the heavens are above the earth.

²⁶"Behold, I set before you this day a blessing and a curse: the
blessing, if you obey the commandments of the LORD your
God, which I command you this day, ²⁸and the curse, if you do
not obey the commandments of the LORD your God, but turn
aside from the way which I command you this day, to go after
other gods which you have not known.

³²"You shall be careful to do all the statutes and the ordinances
which I set before you this day."

SECOND READING

R E Romans 3:21–25a, 28
   L Romans 3:21–25a, 27–28

²¹Now the righteousness of God has been manifested apart
from law, although the law and the prophets bear witness to it,
the righteousness of God through faith in Jesus Christ for all
who believe. For there is no distinction; since all have sinned
and fall short of the glory of God, they are justified by God's
grace as a gift, through the redemption which is in Christ Je-

sus, ^{25a}whom God put forward as an expiation by his blood, ^{25b}to be received by faith.

^{27}Then what becomes of our boasting? It is excluded. On what principle? On the principle of works? No, but on the principle of faith. ^{28}For we hold that the human being is justified by faith apart from works of law.

GOSPEL

R E Matthew 7:21–27
  L Matthew 7:21–29

[At that time Jesus said,]

^{21}"Not every one who says to me, 'Lord, Lord,' shall enter the dominion of heaven, but the one who does the will of my Father who is in heaven. On that day many will say to me, 'Lord, Lord, did we not prophesy in your name, and cast out demons in your name, and do many mighty works in your name?' And then will I declare to them, 'I never knew you; depart from me, you evildoers.'

"Every one then who hears these words of mine and does them will be like a wise man who built his house upon the rock; and the rain fell, and the floods came, and the winds blew and beat upon that house, but it did not fall, because it had been founded on the rock. And every one who hears these words of mine and does not do them will be like a foolish man who built his house upon the sand; ^{27}and the rain fell, and the floods came, and the winds blew and beat against that house, and it fell; and great was the fall of it."

^{28}And when Jesus finished these sayings, the crowds were astonished at his teaching, ^{29}for Jesus taught them as one who had authority, and not as their scribes.

R **TENTH SUNDAY IN ORDINARY TIME**
E **PROPER 5**
L **THIRD SUNDAY AFTER PENTECOST**

FIRST READING

R Hosea 6:3–6
E L Hosea 5:15–6:6

¹⁵I will return again to my place,
  until they acknowledge their guilt and seek my face,
  and in their distress they seek me, saying,
"Come, let us return to the LORD;
  for having torn, the LORD may heal us;
  having stricken, the LORD will bind us up.
After two days the LORD will revive us;
  on the third day the LORD will raise us up,
  that we may live before the face of the LORD.
³Let us know, let us press on to know the LORD,
  whose going forth is sure as the dawn;
the LORD will come to us as the showers,
  as the spring rains that water the earth."
What shall I do with you, O Ephraim?
  What shall I do with you, O Judah?
Your love is like a morning cloud,
  like the dew that goes early away.
Therefore I have hewn them by the prophets,
  I have slain them by the words of my mouth,
  and my judgment goes forth as the light.
⁶For I desire steadfast love and not sacrifice,
  the knowledge of God, rather than burnt offerings.

SECOND READING

R L Romans 4:18–25
E Romans 4:13–18

¹³The promise to Abraham and his descendants, that they
should inherit the world, did not come through the law but
through the righteousness of faith. If it is the adherents of the
law who are to be the heirs, faith is null and the promise is

void. For the law brings wrath, but where there is no law there is no transgression.

That is why it depends on faith, in order that the promise may rest on grace and be guaranteed to all his descendants—not only to the adherents of the law but also to those who share the faith of Abraham, who is the father of us all, as it is written, "I have made you the father of many nations"—in the presence of the God in whom Abraham believed, who gives life to the dead and calls into existence the things that do not exist. [18]In hope Abraham believed against hope, that he should become the father of many nations; as he had been told, "So shall your descendants be." [19]He did not weaken in faith when he considered his own body, which was as good as dead because he was about a hundred years old, or when he considered the barrenness of Sarah's womb. No distrust made Abraham waver concerning the promise of God, but he grew strong in his faith as he gave glory to God, fully convinced that God was able to do what God had promised. That is why his faith was "reckoned to him as righteousness." But the words, "it was reckoned to him," were written not for his sake alone, but for ours also. It will be reckoned to us who believe in the one who raised from the dead Jesus our Lord, [25]who was put to death for our trespasses and raised for our justification.

GOSPEL

R E L   Matthew 9:9–13

[9]Passing on from there, Jesus saw a man called Matthew sitting at the tax office, and said to him, "Follow me." And Matthew rose and followed Jesus.

And as Jesus sat at table in the house, behold, many tax collectors and sinners came and sat down with Jesus and his disciples. And when the Pharisees saw this, they said to his disciples, "Why does your teacher eat with tax collectors and sinners?" But when Jesus heard it, he said, "Those who are well have no need of a physician, but those who are sick. [13]Go and learn what this means, 'I desire mercy, and not sacrifice.' For I came not to call the righteous, but sinners."

R ELEVENTH SUNDAY IN ORDINARY TIME
E PROPER 6
L FOURTH SUNDAY AFTER PENTECOST

FIRST READING

R   Exodus 19:2–6a

E L   Exodus 19:2–8a

²When the people of Israel set out from Rephidim and came into the wilderness of Sinai, they encamped in the wilderness; and there Israel encamped before the mountain. And Moses went up to God, and the LORD called to him out of the mountain, saying, "Thus you shall say to the house of Jacob, and tell the people of Israel: You have seen what I did to the Egyptians, and how I bore you on eagles' wings and brought you to myself. Now therefore, if you will obey my voice and keep my covenant, you shall be my own possession among all peoples; for all the earth is mine, ⁶ᵃand you shall be to me a realm of priests and a holy nation. ⁶ᵇThese are the words which you shall speak to the children of Israel."

So Moses came and called the elders of the people, and set before them all these words which the LORD had commanded him. ⁸ᵃAnd all the people answered together and said, "All that the LORD has spoken we will do."

SECOND READING

R E L   Romans 5:6–11

⁶While we were still weak, at the right time Christ died for the ungodly. Why, one will hardly die for a righteous person—though perhaps for a good person one will dare even to die. But God's own love is shown for us in that while we were yet sinners Christ died for us. Since, therefore, we are now justified by the blood of Christ, much more shall we be saved by him from the wrath of God. For if while we were enemies we were reconciled to God by the death of the Son of God, much more, now that we are reconciled, shall we be saved by the life of the Son of God. ¹¹Not only so, but we also rejoice in God

R   ELEVENTH SUNDAY IN ORDINARY TIME   175
E   PROPER 6
L   FOURTH SUNDAY AFTER PENTECOST

through our Lord Jesus Christ, through whom we have now
received our reconciliation.

GOSPEL

R   Matthew 9:36–10:8
E L   Matthew 9:35–10:8

[35]Jesus went about all the cities and villages, teaching in their
synagogues and preaching the gospel of the dominion of
heaven, and healing every disease and every infirmity. [36]Seeing
the crowds, Jesus had compassion for them, because they were
harassed and helpless, like sheep without a shepherd. Then Jesus said to his disciples, "The harvest is plentiful, but the laborers are few; pray therefore the Lord of the harvest to send
out laborers for the harvesting."

And Jesus summoned his twelve disciples and gave them authority over unclean spirits, to cast them out, and to heal every
disease and every infirmity. The names of the twelve apostles
are these: first, Simon, who is called Peter, and Andrew his
brother; James the son of Zebedee, and John his brother; Philip
and Bartholomew; Thomas and Matthew the tax collector;
James the son of Alphaeus, and Thaddaeus; Simon the Canan-
aean, and Judas Iscariot, who betrayed him.

These twelve Jesus sent out, charging them, "Go nowhere
among the Gentiles, and enter no town of the Samaritans, but
go rather to the lost sheep of the house of Israel. And preach
as you go, saying, 'The dominion of heaven is at hand.' [8]Heal
the sick, raise the dead, cleanse lepers, cast out demons. You
received without paying, give without pay."

R **TWELFTH SUNDAY IN ORDINARY TIME**
E **PROPER 7**
L **FIFTH SUNDAY AFTER PENTECOST**

FIRST READING

R Jeremiah 20:10–13
E L Jeremiah 20:7–13

⁷O LORD, you have deceived me,
  and I was deceived;
you are stronger than I,
  and you have prevailed.
I have become a laughingstock all the day;
  every one mocks me.
For whenever I speak, I cry out,
  I shout, "Violence and destruction!"
For the word of the LORD has become for me
  a reproach and derision all day long.
If I say, "I will not mention the LORD,
  or speak any more in the name of the LORD,"
there is in my heart as it were a burning fire
  shut up in my bones,
and I am weary with holding it in,
  and I cannot.
¹⁰For I hear many whispering.
  Terror is on every side!
"Denounce him! Let us denounce him!"
  say all my familiar friends,
  watching for my fall.
"Perhaps Jeremiah will be deceived,
  then we can overcome him,
  and take our revenge on him."
But the LORD is with me as a dread warrior;
  therefore my persecutors will stumble,
  they will not overcome me.
They will be greatly shamed,
  for they will not succeed.

Their eternal dishonor
    will never be forgotten.
O Lord of hosts, who tries the righteous,
    who sees the heart and the mind,
let me see your vengeance upon them,
    for to you have I committed my cause.
[13]Sing to the Lord;
    praise the Lord!
For the Lord has delivered the life of the needy
    from the hand of evildoers.

SECOND READING

R L   Romans 5:12–15
    E   Romans 5:15b–19

[12]Therefore as sin came into the world through one human being and death through sin, and so death spread to all human
beings because all humans sinned—sin indeed was in the
world before the law was given, but sin is not counted where
there is no law. Yet death reigned from Adam to Moses, even
over those whose sins were not like the transgression of Adam,
who was a type of the one who was to come.

[15a]But the free gift is not like the trespass. [15b]For if many died
through the trespass of one, much more have the grace of God
and the free gift in the grace of that one person Jesus Christ
abounded for many. [16]And the free gift is not like the effect of
that one person's sin. For the judgment following one trespass
brought condemnation, but the free gift following many trespasses brings justification. If, because of the trespass of one,
death reigned through that one, much more will those who receive the abundance of grace and the free gift of righteousness
reign in life through the one Jesus Christ.

Then as the trespass of one led to condemnation for all, so the
act of righteousness of one leads to acquittal and life for all.
[19]For as by the disobedience of one person many were made
sinners, so by the obedience of one person many will be made
righteous.

178   TWELFTH SUNDAY IN ORDINARY TIME   R
    PROPER 7   E
    FIFTH SUNDAY AFTER PENTECOST   L

GOSPEL

R   Matthew 10:26–33
E L   Matthew 10:24–33

[At that time Jesus said,]

24"The disciple is not above the teacher, nor the slave above the master; it is enough for the disciple to be like the teacher, and the slave like the master. If they have called the master of the house Beelzebul, how much more will they malign those of Beelzebul's household.

26"So have no fear of them; for nothing is covered that will not be revealed, or hidden that will not be known. What I tell you in the dark, utter in the light; and what you hear whispered, proclaim upon the housetops. And do not fear those who kill the body but cannot kill the soul; rather fear the one who can destroy both soul and body in hell. Are not two sparrows sold for a penny? And not one of them will fall to the ground without your Father's will. But even the hairs of your head are all numbered. Fear not, therefore; you are of more value than many sparrows. So every one who acknowledges me before others, I also will acknowledge before my Father who is in heaven; 33but whoever denies me before others, I also will deny before my Father who is in heaven."

R THIRTEENTH SUNDAY IN ORDINARY TIME

E PROPER 8

L SIXTH SUNDAY AFTER PENTECOST

FIRST READING

R   2 Kings 4:8–11, 14–16a

⁸One day Elisha went onto Shunem, where a wealthy woman lived, who urged him to eat some food. So whenever he passed that way, he would turn in there to eat food. And she said to her husband, "Behold now, I perceive that this is a holy man of God, who is continually passing our way. Let us make a small roof chamber with walls, and put there for him a bed, a table, a chair, and a lamp, so that whenever he comes to us, he can go in there."

¹¹One day he came there, and he turned into the chamber and rested there. ¹⁴And Elisha said, "What then is to be done for her?" Gehazi answered, "Well, she has no son, and her husband is old." He said, "Call her." And when he had called her, she stood in the doorway. ¹⁶ᵃAnd he said, "At this season, when the time comes round, you shall embrace a son."

E   Isaiah 2:10–17

¹⁰Enter into the rock,
    and hide in the dust
from before the terror of the LORD,
    and from the glory of God's majesty.
The haughty looks of a human being shall be brought low,
    and human pride shall be humbled;
and the LORD alone will be exalted in that day.
For the LORD of hosts has a day
    against all that is proud and lofty,
    against all that is lifted up and high;
against all the cedars of Lebanon,
    lofty and lifted up;
    and against all the oaks of Bashan;
against all the high mountains,
    and against all lofty hills;

against every high tower,
    and against every fortified wall;
against all the ships of Tarshish,
    and against all the beautiful craft.
¹⁷And the haughtiness of the human being shall be humbled,
    and human pride shall be brought low;
    and the LORD alone will be exalted in that day.

L   Jeremiah 28:5–9

⁵Then the prophet Jeremiah spoke to Hananiah the prophet in the presence of the priests and all the people who were standing in the house of the LORD; and the prophet Jeremiah said, "Amen! May the LORD do so; may the LORD make the words which you have prophesied come true, and bring back to this place from Babylon the vessels of the house of the LORD, and all the exiles. Yet hear now this word which I speak in your hearing and in the hearing of all the people. The prophets who preceded you and me from ancient times prophesied war, famine, and pestilence against many countries and great realms. ⁹As for the prophet who prophesies peace, when the word of that prophet comes to pass, then it will be known that the LORD has truly sent the prophet."

SECOND READING

R   Romans 6:3–4, 8–11
E   Romans 6:3–11
L   Romans 6:1b–11

¹ᵇAre we to continue in sin that grace may abound? By no means! How can we who died to sin still live in it? ³Do you not know that all of us who have been baptized into Christ Jesus were baptized into his death? ⁴We were buried therefore with Christ by baptism into death, so that as Christ was raised from the dead by the glory of the Father, we too might walk in newness of life.

⁵For if we have been united with Christ in a death like his, we shall certainly be united with him in a resurrection like his. We know that our old self was crucified with Christ so that the sinful body might be destroyed, and we might no longer be

R   THIRTEENTH SUNDAY IN ORDINARY TIME   181
E   PROPER 8
L   SIXTH SUNDAY AFTER PENTECOST

enslaved to sin. For the one who has died is freed from sin. [8]But if we have died with Christ, we believe that we shall also live with him. For we know that Christ being raised from the dead will never die again; death no longer has dominion over him. The death he died he died to sin, once for all, but the life he lives he lives to God. [11]So you also must consider yourselves dead to sin and alive to God in Christ Jesus.

GOSPEL

R   Matthew 10:37–42

E L Matthew 10:34–42

[At that time Jesus said,]

[34]"Do not think that I have come to bring peace on earth; I have not come to bring peace, but a sword. For I have come to set a son against his father, and a daughter against her mother, and a daughter-in-law against her mother-in-law; and people's foes will be those of their own household. [37]They who love father or mother more than me are not worthy of me; and they who love son or daughter more than me are not worthy of me; and those who do not take their cross and follow me are not worthy of me. They who find their life will lose it, and they who lose their life for my sake will find it.

"Those who receive you receive me, and those who receive me receive the one who sent me. Those who receive a prophet as a prophet shall receive a prophet's reward, and those who receive one who is righteous as righteous shall receive the reward of the righteous. [42]And those who give to one of these little ones even a cup of cold water because that little one is a disciple, truly, I say to you, they shall not lose their reward."

R FOURTEENTH SUNDAY IN ORDINARY TIME
E PROPER 9
L SEVENTH SUNDAY AFTER PENTECOST

FIRST READING

R Zechariah 9:9–10
E L Zechariah 9:9–12

⁹Rejoice greatly, O daughter Zion!
  Shout aloud, O daughter Jerusalem!
Lo, your king comes to you;
  triumphant and victorious is he,
humble and riding on a donkey,
  on a colt the foal of a donkey.
¹⁰I will cut off the chariot from Ephraim
  and the war horse from Jerusalem;
and the battle bow shall be cut off,
  and the king shall command peace to the nations;
his dominion shall be from sea to sea,
  and from the River to the ends of the earth.
¹¹As for you also, because of the blood of my covenant with
    you,
  I will set your captives free from the waterless pit,
¹²Return to your stronghold, O prisoners of hope;
  today I declare that I will restore you double.

SECOND READING

R Romans 8:9, 11–13

⁹But you are not in the flesh, you are in the Spirit, if in fact the
Spirit of God dwells in you. Any one who does not have the
Spirit of Christ does not belong to Christ. ¹¹If the Spirit of the
one who raised Jesus from the dead dwells in you, the one
who raised Christ Jesus from the dead will give life to your
mortal bodies also through this Spirit dwelling in you.

So then, my dear people, we are debtors, not to the flesh, to
live according to the flesh—¹³for if you live according to the
flesh you will die, but if by the Spirit you put to death the
deeds of the body you will live.

E   Romans 7:21–8:6
L   Romans 7:15–25a

[15]I do not understand my own actions. For I do not do what I want, but I do the very thing I hate. Now if I do what I do not want, I agree that the law is good. So then it is no longer I that do it, but sin which dwells within me. For I know that nothing good dwells within me, that is, in my flesh. I can will what is right, but I cannot do it. For I do not do the good I want, but the evil I do not want is what I do. Now if I do what I do not want, it is no longer I that do it, but sin which dwells within me.

[21]So I find it to be a law that when I want to do right, evil lies close at hand. For I delight in the law of God, in my inmost self, but I see in my physical body another law at war with the law of my mind and making me captive to the law of sin which dwells in my physical body. Wretched man that I am! Who will deliver me from this body of death? [25a]Thanks be to God through Jesus Christ our Lord! [25b]So then, I of myself serve the law of God with my mind, but with my flesh I serve the law of sin.

There is therefore now no condemnation for those who are in Christ Jesus. For the law of the Spirit of life in Christ Jesus has set me free from the law of sin and death. For God has done what the law, weakened by the flesh, could not do: sending God's own Son in the likeness of sinful flesh and for sin, God condemned sin in the flesh, in order that the just requirement of the law might be fulfilled in us, who walk not according to the flesh but according to the Spirit. For those who live according to the flesh set their minds on the things of the flesh, but those who live according to the Spirit set their minds on the things of the Spirit. [6]To set the mind on the flesh is death, but to set the mind on the Spirit is life and peace.

GOSPEL

R   E   L   Matthew 11:25–30

[25]At that time Jesus declared, "I thank you, Father, Lord of heaven and earth, that you have hidden these things from the wise and understanding and revealed them to infants; yes,

Father, for such was your gracious will. All things have been delivered to me by my Father; and no one knows the Son except the Father, and no one knows the Father except the Son and any one to whom the Son chooses to reveal the Father. Come to me, all who labor and are heavy laden, and I will give you rest. Take my yoke upon you, and learn from me; for I am gentle and lowly in heart, and you will find rest for your souls. [30]For my yoke is easy, and my burden is light."

FIRST READING

R L Isaiah 55:10–11
E   Isaiah 55:1–5, 10–13

[1]"Ho, every one who thirsts,
   come to the waters;
and whoever has no money,
   come, buy and eat!
Come, buy wine and milk
   without money and without price.
Why do you spend your money for that which is not bread,
   and your labor for that which does not satisfy?
Hearken diligently to me, and eat what is good,
   and delight yourselves in fatness.
Incline your ear, and come to me;
   hear, that your soul may live;
and I will make with you an everlasting covenant,
   my steadfast, sure love for David.
Behold, I made him a witness to the peoples,
   a leader and commander for the peoples.
[5]Behold, you shall call nations that you know not,
   and nations that knew you not shall run to you,
because of the LORD your God, and of the Holy One of Israel,
   for the LORD has glorified you.
[10]For as the rain and the snow come down from heaven,
   and return not thither but water the earth,
making it bring forth and sprout,
   giving seed to the sower and bread to the eater,
[11]so shall my word be that goes forth from my mouth;
   it shall not return to me empty,
but it shall accomplish that which I purpose,
   and prosper in the thing for which I sent it.
[12]For you shall go out in joy,
   and be led forth in peace;

the mountains and the hills before you
   shall break forth into singing,
   and all the trees of the field shall clap their hands.
¹³Instead of the thorn shall come up the cypress;
   instead of the brier shall come up the myrtle;
and it shall be to the LORD for a memorial,
   for an everlasting sign which shall not be cut off."

SECOND READING

R   Romans 8:18–23
L   Romans 8:18–25

¹⁸I consider that the sufferings of this present time are not
worth comparing with the glory that is to be revealed to us. For
the creation waits with eager longing for the revealing of the
children of God; for the creation was subjected to futility, not
of its own will but by the will of the one who subjected it in
hope; because the creation itself will be set free from its bondage to decay and obtain the glorious liberty of the children of
God. We know that the whole creation has been groaning in
labor pangs together until now; ²³and not only the creation, but
we ourselves, who have the first fruits of the Spirit, groan inwardly as we wait for adoption, the redemption of our bodies.
²⁴For in this hope we were saved. Now hope that is seen is not
hope. For who hopes for what is seen? ²⁵But if we hope for
what we do not see, we wait for it with patience.

E   Romans 8:9–17

⁹But you are not in the flesh, you are in the Spirit, if in fact the
Spirit of God dwells in you. Any one who does not have the
Spirit of Christ does not belong to Christ. But if Christ is in
you, although your bodies are dead because of sin, your spirits
are alive because of righteousness. If the Spirit of the one who
raised Jesus from the dead dwells in you, the one who raised
Christ Jesus from the dead will give life to your mortal bodies
also through this Spirit dwelling in you.

So then, my dear people, we are debtors, not to the flesh, to
live according to the flesh—for if you live according to the flesh

you will die, but if by the Spirit you put to death the deeds of the body you will live. For all who are led by the Spirit of God are children of God. For you did not receive the spirit of slavery to fall back into fear, but you have received the spirit of adoption. When we cry, "Abba! Father!" it is that very Spirit bearing witness with our spirit that we are children of God, 17and if children, then heirs, heirs of God and joint heirs with Christ, provided we suffer with Christ in order that we may also be glorified with Christ.

GOSPEL

R Matthew 13:1–23
E Matthew 13:1–9, 18–23
L Matthew 13:1–9

1That same day Jesus went out of the house and sat beside the sea. And great crowds gathered about him, so that he got into a boat and sat there; and the whole crowd stood on the beach. And Jesus told them many things in parables, saying: "A sower went out to sow. And in sowing, some seeds fell along the path, and the birds came and devoured them. Other seeds fell on rocky ground, where they had not much soil, and immediately they sprang up, since they had no depth of soil, but when the sun rose they were scorched; and since they had no root they withered away. Other seeds fell upon thorns, and the thorns grew up and choked them. Other seeds fell on good soil and brought forth grain, some a hundredfold, some sixty, some thirty. 9Let the one with ears hear!"

10Then the disciples came and said to Jesus, "Why do you speak to them in parables? And Jesus answered them, "To you it has been given to know the secrets of the dominion of heaven, but to them it has not been given. For to them who have will more be given, and they will have abundance; but from them who have not, even what they have will be taken away. This is why I speak to them in parables, because seeing they do not see, and hearing they do not hear, nor do they understand. With them indeed is fulfilled the prophecy of Isaiah which says:

'You shall indeed hear but never understand,
and you shall indeed see but never perceive.
For this people's heart has grown dull,
and their ears are heavy of hearing,
and their eyes they have closed,
lest they should perceive with their eyes,
and hear with their ears,
and understand with their heart,
and turn for me to heal them.'

But blessed are your eyes, for they see, and your ears, for they hear. Truly, I say to you, many prophets and righteous people longed to see what you see, and did not see it, and to hear what you hear, and did not hear it.

[18]"Hear then the parable of the sower. When people hear the word of the dominion of heaven and do not understand it, the evil one comes and snatches away what is sown in their hearts; this is what was sown along the path. As for what was sown on rocky ground, this is they who hear the word and immediately receive it with joy; yet they have no root in themselves, but endure for a while, and when tribulation or persecution arises on account of the word, immediately they fall away. As for what was sown among thorns, this is they who hear the word, but the cares of the world and the delight in riches choke the word, and it proves unfruitful. [23]As for what was sown on good soil, this is they who hear the word and understand it; they indeed bear fruit, and yield, in one case a hundredfold, in another sixty, and in another thirty."

R SIXTEENTH SUNDAY IN ORDINARY TIME

E PROPER 11

L NINTH SUNDAY AFTER PENTECOST

FIRST READING

R E Wisdom 12:13, 16–19

¹³There is no god besides you, whose care is for all,
to whom you should prove that you have not judged unjustly.
¹⁶For your strength is the source of righteousness,
and your sovereignty over all causes you to spare all.
For you show your strength when the completeness of your
    power is doubted,
and you rebuke any insolence among those who know it.
You who are sovereign in strength judge with mildness,
and with great forbearance you govern us;
for you have power to act whenever you choose.
¹⁹Through such works you have taught your people
that those who are righteous must be kind,
and you have filled your children with good hope,
because you give repentance for sins.

L Isaiah 44:6–8

⁶Thus says the LORD, the Sovereign of Israel
    and Israel's Redeemer, the LORD of hosts:
"I am the first and I am the last;
    besides me there is no god.
If any is like me, O, then, proclaim it,
    and declare it and set it forth before me.
Who has announced from of old the things to come?
    Let them tell us what is yet to be.
⁸Fear not, nor be afraid;
    have I not told you from of old and declared it?
    And you are my witnesses!
Is there a God besides me?
    There is no Rock; I know not any."

SECOND READING

R L   Romans 8:26–27

[26]The Spirit helps us in our weakness; for we do not know how to pray as we ought, but that very Spirit intercedes for us with sighs too deep for words. [27]And the one who searches human hearts knows what is the mind of the Spirit, because the Spirit intercedes for the saints according to the will of God.

E   Romans 8:18–25

[18]I consider that the sufferings of this present time are not worth comparing with the glory that is to be revealed to us. For the creation waits with eager longing for the revealing of the children of God; for the creation was subjected to futility, not of its own will but by the will of the one who subjected it in hope; because the creation itself will be set free from its bondage to decay and obtain the glorious liberty of the children of God. We know that the whole creation has been groaning in labor pangs together until now; and not only the creation, but we ourselves, who have the first fruits of the Spirit, groan inwardly as we wait for adoption, the redemption of our bodies. For in this hope we were saved. Now hope that is seen is not hope. For who hopes for what is seen? [25]But if we hope for what we do not see, we wait for it with patience.

GOSPEL

R   Matthew 13:24–43
E   Matthew 13:24–30, 36–43
L   Matthew 13:24–30

[24]Another parable Jesus put before them, saying, "The dominion of heaven may be compared to someone who sowed good seed in his field; but while people slept, his enemy came and sowed weeds among the wheat, and went away. So when the plants came up and bore grain, then the weeds appeared also. And the slaves of the householder came and said to him, 'Sir, did you not sow good seed in your field? How then has it weeds?' He said to them, 'An enemy has done this.' The slaves said to him, 'Then do you want us to go and gather them?' But the householder said, 'No; lest in gathering the weeds you root

R   SIXTEENTH SUNDAY IN ORDINARY TIME   191
E   PROPER 11
L   NINTH SUNDAY AFTER PENTECOST

up the wheat along with them. ³⁰Let both grow together until the harvest; and at harvest time I will tell the reapers, Gather the weeds first and bind them in bundles to be burned, but gather the wheat into my barn.' "

³¹Another parable Jesus put before them, saying, "The dominion of heaven is like a grain of mustard seed which someone took and sowed in his field; it is the smallest of all seeds, but when it has grown it is the greatest of shrubs and becomes a tree, so that the birds of the air come and make nests in its branches."

Jesus told them another parable. "The dominion of heaven is like leaven which a woman took and hid in three measures of flour, till it was all leavened."

All this Jesus said to the crowds in parables; indeed he said nothing to them without a parable. This was to fulfill what was spoken by the prophet:

"I will open my mouth in parables,
I will utter what has been hidden since the foundation of the
    world."

³⁶Then Jesus left the crowds and went into the house. And his disciples came to him, saying, "Explain to us the parable of the weeds of the field." Jesus answered, "The one who sows the good seed is the Man of Heaven; the field is the world, and the good seed means the children of God's dominion; the weeds are the children of the evil one, and the enemy who sowed them is the devil; the harvest is the close of the age, and the reapers are angels. Just as the weeds are gathered and burned with fire, so will it be at the close of the age. The Man of Heaven will send his angels, and they will gather out of his dominion all causes of sin and all evildoers, and throw them into the furnace of fire; there they shall weep and gnash their teeth. ⁴³Then the righteous will shine like the sun in the dominion of their Father. Let the one with ears hear!"

R SEVENTEENTH SUNDAY IN ORDINARY TIME
E PROPER 12
L TENTH SUNDAY AFTER PENTECOST

FIRST READING

R   1 Kings 3:5, 7–12
E L   1 Kings 3:5–12

5At Gibeon the LORD appeared to Solomon in a dream by night; and God said, "Ask what I shall give you." 6And Solomon said, "You have shown great and steadfast love to your servant David my father, because he walked before you in faithfulness, in righteousness, and in uprightness of heart toward you; and you have kept for him this great and steadfast love, and have given him a son to sit on his throne this day. 7And now, O LORD my God, you have made your servant king in place of David my father, although I am but a little child; I do not know how to go out or come in. And your servant is in the midst of your people whom you have chosen, a great people, that cannot be numbered or counted for multitude. Give your servant therefore an understanding mind to govern your people, that I may discern between good and evil; for who is able to govern this your great people?"

It pleased the Lord that Solomon had asked this. And God said to Solomon, "Because you have asked this, and have not asked for yourself long life or riches or the life of your enemies, but have asked for yourself understanding to discern what is right, 12behold, I now do according to your word. Behold, I give you a wise and discerning mind, so that none like you has been before you and none like you shall rise after you."

SECOND READING

R L   Romans 8:28–30
E   Romans 8:26–34

26The Spirit helps us in our weakness; for we do not know how to pray as we ought, but that very Spirit intercedes for us with sighs too deep for words. And the one who searches human hearts knows what is the mind of the Spirit, because the Spirit intercedes for the saints according to the will of God.

[28]We know that in everything God works for good with those who love God, who are called according to the divine purpose. For those whom God foreknew God also predestined to be conformed to the image of the Son of God, in order that the Son might be the first-born among many children. [30]And those whom God predestined God also called; and those whom God called God also justified; and those whom God justified God also glorified.

[31]What then shall we say to this? If God is for us, who is against us? God did not spare God's own Son, but gave him up for us all; how shall God then not give us all things, along with the Son? Who shall bring any charge against God's elect? It is God who justifies; [34]who is to condemn? Is it Christ Jesus, who died, yes, who was raised from the dead, who is at the right hand of God, who indeed intercedes for us?

GOSPEL

R L   Matthew 13:44–52
   E   Matthew 13:31–33, 44–49a

[31]Another parable Jesus put before them, saying, "The dominion of heaven is like a grain of mustard seed which someone took and sowed in his field; it is the smallest of all seeds, but when it has grown it is the greatest of shrubs and becomes a tree, so that the birds of the air come and make nests in its branches."

[33]Jesus told them another parable. "The dominion of heaven is like leaven which a woman took and hid in three measures of flour, till it was all leavened."

[44]"The dominion of heaven is like treasure hidden in a field, which someone found and covered up; then in his joy he goes and sells all that he has and buys that field.

"Again, the dominion of heaven is like a merchant in search of fine pearls, who, on finding one pearl of great value, went and sold all that he had and bought it.

"Again, the dominion of heaven is like a net which was thrown into the sea and gathered fish of every kind; when it was full, people drew it ashore and sat down and sorted the good into vessels but threw away the bad. [49a]So it will be at the close of the age. [49b]The angels will come out and separate the evil from the righteous, and throw them into the furnace of fire; there they will weep and gnash their teeth.

"Have you understood all this?" They said to Jesus, "Yes." [52]And Jesus said to them, "Therefore every scribe who has been trained for the dominion of heaven is like a householder who brings out of the household treasure what is new and what is old."

R **EIGHTEENTH SUNDAY IN ORDINARY TIME**
E **PROPER 13**
L **ELEVENTH SUNDAY AFTER PENTECOST**

FIRST READING

R   Isaiah 55:1–3
L   Isaiah 55:1–5

¹"Ho, every one who thirsts,
    come to the waters;
and whoever has no money,
    come, buy and eat!
Come, buy wine and milk
    without money and without price.
Why do you spend your money for that which is not bread,
    and your labor for that which does not satisfy?
Hearken diligently to me, and eat what is good,
    and delight yourselves in fatness.
³Incline your ear, and come to me;
    hear, that your soul may live;
and I will make with you an everlasting covenant,
    my steadfast, sure love for David.
⁴Behold, I made him a witness to the peoples,
    a leader and commander for the peoples.
⁵Behold, you shall call nations that you know not,
    and nations that knew you not shall run to you,
because of the LORD your God, and of the Holy One of Israel,
    for the LORD has glorified you."

E   Nehemiah 9:16–20

¹⁶"Our forebears acted presumptuously and stiffened their neck
and did not obey your commandments; they refused to obey,
and were not mindful of the wonders which you performed
among them; but they stiffened their neck and appointed a
leader to return to their bondage in Egypt. But you are a God
ready to forgive, gracious and merciful, slow to anger and
abounding in steadfast love, and did not forsake them. Even
when they had made for themselves a molten calf and said,
'This is your God who brought you up out of Egypt,' and had

196 EIGHTEENTH SUNDAY IN ORDINARY TIME   R
      PROPER 13   E
      ELEVENTH SUNDAY AFTER PENTECOST   L

committed great blasphemies, you in your great mercies did not forsake them in the wilderness; the pillar of cloud which led them in the way did not depart from them by day, nor the pillar of fire by night which lighted for them the way by which they should go. [20]You gave your good Spirit to instruct them, and did not withhold your manna from their mouth, and gave them water for their thirst."

SECOND READING

R Romans 8: 35, 37–39
E L Romans 8:35–39

[35]Who shall separate us from the love of Christ? Shall tribulation, or distress, or persecution, or famine, or nakedness, or peril, or sword? [36]As it is written,

'For your sake we are being killed all the day long;
we are regarded as sheep to be slaughtered.'

[37]No, in all these things we are more than conquerors through the one who loved us. For I am sure that neither death, nor life, nor angels, nor principalities, nor things present, nor things to come, nor powers, [39]nor height, nor depth, nor anything else in all creation, will be able to separate us from the love of God in Christ Jesus our Lord.

GOSPEL

R E L Matthew 14:13–21

[13]When Jesus heard this, he withdrew from there in a boat to a lonely place apart. But when the crowds heard it, they followed him on foot from the towns. And going ashore Jesus saw a great throng; and he had compassion on them, and healed their sick. When it was evening, the disciples came to him and said, "This is a lonely place, and the day is now over; send the crowds away to go into the villages and buy food for themselves." Jesus said, "They need not go away; you give them something to eat." They said to him, "We have only five loaves here and two fish." And Jesus said, "Bring them here to me." Then Jesus ordered the crowds to sit down on the grass; and

taking the five loaves and the two fish Jesus looked up to heaven, and blessed, and broke and gave the loaves to the disciples, and the disciples gave them to the crowds. And they all ate and were satisfied. And they took up twelve baskets full of the broken pieces left over. [21]And those who ate were about five thousand men, besides women and children.

FIRST READING

R 1 Kings 19:9a, 11–13a
L 1 Kings 19:9–18

⁹ᵃElijah came to a cave, and lodged there; ⁹ᵇand behold, the word of the LORD came to him, and said to him, "What are you doing here, Elijah?" Elijah said, "I have been very jealous for the LORD, the God of hosts; for the people of Israel have forsaken your covenant, thrown down your altars, and slain your prophets with the sword; and I, even I only, am left; and they seek my life, to take it away." ¹¹And the LORD said, "Go forth, and stand upon the mount before the LORD." And behold, the LORD passed by, and a great and strong wind rent the mountains, and broke in pieces the rocks before the LORD, but the LORD was not in the wind; and after the wind an earthquake, but the LORD was not in the earthquake; and after the earthquake a fire, but the LORD was not in the fire; and after the fire a still small voice. ¹³ᵃAnd when Elijah heard it, he wrapped his face in his mantle and went out and stood at the entrance of the cave. ¹³ᵇAnd behold, there came a voice to him, and said, "What are you doing here, Elijah?" He said, "I have been very jealous for the LORD, the God of hosts; for the people of Israel have forsaken your covenant, thrown down your altars, and slain your prophets with the sword; and I, even I only, am left; and they seek my life, to take it away." And the LORD said to him, "Go, return on your way to the wilderness of Damascus; and when you arrive, you shall anoint Hazael to be king over Syria; and Jehu the son of Nimshi you shall anoint to be king over Israel; and Elisha the son of Shaphat of Abelmeholah you shall anoint to be prophet in your place. And the one who escapes from the sword of Hazael shall Jehu slay; and the one who escapes from the sword of Jehu shall Elisha slay. ¹⁸Yet I will leave seven thousand in Israel, all the knees that have not bowed to Baal, and every mouth that has not kissed him."

E Jonah 2:1–9

¹Then Jonah prayed to the Lord his God from the belly of the
fish, saying,
"I called to the Lord, out of my distress,
    and the Lord answered me;
out of the belly of Sheol I cried,
    and you heard my voice.
For you cast me into the deep,
    into the heart of the seas,
    and the flood was round about me;
all your waves and your billows
    passed over me.
Then I said, 'I am cast out
    from your presence;
how shall I again look
    upon your holy temple?'
The waters closed in over me,
    the deep was round about me;
weeds were wrapped about my head
    at the roots of the mountains.
I went down to the land
    whose bars closed upon me for ever;
yet you brought up my life from the Pit,
    O Lord my God.
When my soul fainted within me,
    I remembered the Lord;
and my prayer came to you,
    into your holy temple.
Those who pay regard to vain idols
    forsake their true loyalty.
⁹But I with the voice of thanksgiving
    will sacrifice to you;
what I have vowed I will pay.
    Deliverance belongs to the Lord!"

SECOND READING

R E L Romans 9:1–5

¹I am speaking the truth in Christ, I am not lying; my conscience bears me witness in the Holy Spirit, that I have great sorrow and unceasing anguish in my heart. For I could wish that I myself were accursed and cut off from Christ for the sake of my people, my kin by race. They are Israelites, and to them belong the adoption, the glory, the covenants, the giving of the law, the worship, and the promises; ⁵to them belong the patriarchs, and of their race, according to the flesh, is the Christ. God who is over all be blessed for ever. Amen.

GOSPEL

R E L Matthew 14:22–33

²²Jesus made the disciples get into the boat and go before him to the other side, while he dismissed the crowds. And having dismissed the crowds, Jesus went up on the mountain by himself to pray. When evening came, he was there alone, but the boat by this time was many furlongs distant from the land, beaten by the waves; for the wind was against them. And in the fourth watch of the night Jesus came to them, walking on the sea. But when the disciples saw Jesus walking on the sea, they were terrified, saying, "It is a ghost!" And they cried out for fear. But immediately Jesus spoke to them, saying, "Take heart, it is I; have no fear."

And Peter answered Jesus, "Lord, if it is you, bid me come to you on the water." Jesus said, "Come." So Peter got out of the boat and walked on the water and came to Jesus; but when he saw the wind, he was afraid, and beginning to sink he cried out, "Lord, save me." Jesus immediately reached out his hand and caught him, saying to him, "O you of little faith, why did you doubt?" And when they got into the boat, the wind ceased. ³³And those in the boat worshiped Jesus, saying, "Truly you are the Son of God."

R TWENTIETH SUNDAY IN ORDINARY TIME

E PROPER 15

L THIRTEENTH SUNDAY AFTER PENTECOST

FIRST READING

R E Isaiah 56:1, 6–7

L Isaiah 56:1, 6–8

¹Thus says the LORD:
   "Keep justice, and do righteousness,
for soon my salvation will come,
   and my deliverance be revealed.
⁶And the foreigners who join themselves to the LORD,
   to minister to the LORD, to love the name of the LORD,
   and to be the LORD's servants,
every one who keeps the sabbath, and does not profane it,
   and holds fast my covenant—
⁷these I will bring to my holy mountain,
   and make them joyful in my house of prayer;
their burnt offerings and their sacrifices
   will be accepted on my altar;
for my house shall be called a house of prayer
   for all peoples.
⁸Thus says the Lord GOD,
   who gathers the outcasts of Israel,
I will gather yet others to Israel
   besides those already gathered."

SECOND READING

R E L Romans 11:13–15, 29–32

¹³Now I am speaking to you Gentiles. Inasmuch then as I am an apostle to the Gentiles, I magnify my ministry in order to make Israel, my kin, jealous, and thus save some of them. ¹⁵For if their rejection means the reconciliation of the world, what will their acceptance mean but life from the dead?

²⁹For the gifts and the call of God are irrevocable. Just as you were once disobedient to God but now have received mercy

because of their disobedience, so they have now been disobedient in order that by the mercy shown to you they also may receive mercy. ³²For God has consigned everyone to disobedience, in order to have mercy upon all.

GOSPEL

R E L Matthew 15:21–28

²¹Jesus went away from there and withdrew to the district of Tyre and Sidon. And behold, a Canaanite woman from that region came out and cried, "Have mercy on me, O Lord, Son of David; my daughter is severely possessed by a demon." But Jesus did not answer her a word. And his disciples came and begged him, saying, "Send her away, for she is crying after us." Jesus answered, "I was sent only to the lost sheep of the house of Israel." But she came and knelt before him, saying, "Lord, help me." And Jesus answered, "It is not fair to take the children's bread and throw it to the dogs." She said, "Yes, Lord, yet even the dogs eat the crumbs that fall from their masters' table." ²⁸Then Jesus answered her, "O woman, great is your faith! Be it done for you as you desire." And her daughter was healed instantly.

FIRST READING

R Isaiah 22: 19–23

¹⁹"I will thrust you from your office, and you will be cast down from your station. In that day I will call my servant Eliakim the son of Hilkiah, and I will clothe him with your robe, and will bind your belt around him, and will commit your authority to his hand; and he shall be as a father to the inhabitants of Jerusalem and to the house of Judah. And I will place on his shoulder the key of the house of David; he shall open, and none shall shut; and he shall shut, and none shall open. ²³And I will fasten him like a peg in a sure place, and he will become a throne of honor to his family."

E Isaiah 51:1–6

¹"Hearken to me, you who pursue deliverance,
   you who seek the LORD;
look to the rock from which you were hewn,
   and to the quarry from which you were digged.
Look to Abraham your father
   and to Sarah who bore you;
for when Abraham was but one I called him,
   and I blessed him and made him many.
For the LORD will comfort Zion,
   comfort all its waste places,
and will make its wilderness like Eden,
   its desert like the garden of the LORD;
joy and gladness will be found in Zion,
   thanksgiving and the voice of song.
Listen to me, my people,
   and give ear to me, my nation;
for a law will go forth from me,
   and my justice for a light to the peoples.
My deliverance draws near speedily,
   my salvation has gone forth,
   and my arms will rule the peoples;

the coastlands wait for me,
   and for my arm they hope.
⁶Lift up your eyes to the heavens,
   and look at the earth beneath;
for the heavens will vanish like smoke,
   the earth will wear out like a garment,
   and they who dwell in it will die like gnats;
but my salvation will be for ever,
   and my deliverance will never be ended."

L   Exodus 6:2–8

²God said to Moses, "I am the LORD. I appeared to Abraham,
to Isaac, and to Jacob, as God Almighty, but by my name the
LORD I did not make myself known to them. I also established
my covenant with them, to give them the land of Canaan, the
land in which they dwelt as sojourners. Moreover I have heard
the groaning of the people of Israel whom the Egyptians hold
in bondage and I have remembered my covenant. Say therefore
to the people of Israel, 'I am the LORD, and I will bring you
out from under the burdens of the Egyptians, and I will deliver
you from their bondage, and I will redeem you with an out-
stretched arm and with great acts of judgment, and I will take
you for my people, and I will be your God; and you shall know
that I am the LORD your God, who has brought you out from
under the burdens of the Egyptians. ⁸And I will bring you into
the land which I swore to give to Abraham, to Isaac, and to
Jacob; I will give it to you for a possession. I am the LORD.' "

SECOND READING

R E L   Romans 11:33–36

³³O the depth of the riches and wisdom and knowledge of God!
How unsearchable are God's judgments and how inscrutable
God's ways!

"For who has known the mind of the Lord,
or who has been the Lord's counselor?"
"Or who has given a gift to God
that would require repayment?"

³⁶For from God and through God and to God are all things, to
whom be glory for ever. Amen.

GOSPEL

R E L Matthew 16:13–20

¹³When Jesus came into the district of Caesarea Philippi, he asked his disciples, "Who do people say that the Man of Heaven is?" And they said, "Some say John the Baptist, others say Elijah, and others Jeremiah or one of the prophets." Jesus said to them, "But who do you say that I am?" Simon Peter replied, "You are the Christ, the Son of the living God." And Jesus answered him, "Blessed are you, Simon Bar-Jona! For flesh and blood has not revealed this to you, but my Father who is in heaven. And I tell you, you are Peter, and on this rock I will build my church, and the powers of death shall not prevail against it. I will give you the keys of the dominion of heaven, and whatever you bind on earth shall be bound in heaven, and whatever you loose on earth shall be loosed in heaven." ²⁰Then Jesus strictly charged the disciples to tell no one that he was the Christ.

R   TWENTY-SECOND SUNDAY IN ORDINARY TIME
E   PROPER 17
L   FIFTEENTH SUNDAY AFTER PENTECOST

FIRST READING

R   Jeremiah 20:7–9

> [7]O Lord, you have deceived me,
>   and I was deceived;
> you are stronger than I,
>   and you have prevailed.
> I have become a laughingstock all the day;
>   every one mocks me.
> For whenever I speak, I cry out,
>   I shout, "Violence and destruction!"
> For the word of the Lord has become for me
>   a reproach and derision all day long.
> [9]If I say, "I will not mention the Lord,
>   or speak any more in the Lord's name,"
> there is in my heart as it were a burning fire
>   shut up in my bones,
> and I am weary with holding it in,
>   and I cannot.

E L   Jeremiah 15:15–21

> [15]O Lord, you know;
>   remember me and visit me,
>   and take vengeance for me on my persecutors.
> In your forbearance take me not away;
>   know that for your sake I bear reproach.
> Your words were found, and I ate them,
>   and your words became to me a joy
>   and the delight of my heart;
> for I am called by your name,
>   O Lord, God of hosts.
> I did not sit in the company of merrymakers,
>   nor did I rejoice;
> I sat alone, because your hand was upon me,
>   for you had filled me with indignation.

R   TWENTY-SECOND SUNDAY IN ORDINARY TIME   207
E   PROPER 17
L   FIFTEENTH SUNDAY AFTER PENTECOST

Why is my pain unceasing,
  my wound incurable,
    refusing to be healed?
Will you be to me like a deceitful brook,
  like waters that fail?
Therefore thus says the LORD:
"If you return, I will restore you,
  and you shall stand before me.
If you utter what is precious, and not what is worthless,
  you shall be as my mouth.
They shall turn to you,
  but you shall not turn to them.
And I will make you to this people
  a fortified wall of bronze;
they will fight against you,
  but they shall not prevail over you,
for I am with you
  to save you and deliver you, says the LORD.
²¹I will deliver you out of the hand of the wicked,
  and redeem you from the grasp of the ruthless."

SECOND READING

R   Romans 12:1–2
E L   Romans 12:1–8

¹I appeal to you therefore, my dear people, by the mercies of
God, to present your bodies as a living sacrifice, holy and acceptable to God, which is your spiritual worship. ²Do not be
conformed to this world but be transformed by the renewal of
your mind, that you may prove what is the will of God, what
is good and acceptable and perfect.

³For by the grace given to me I bid every one among you not to
think of yourself more highly than you ought to think, but to
think with sober judgment, each according to the measure of
faith which God has assigned you. For as in one body we have
many parts, and all the parts do not have the same function, so
we, though many, are one body in Christ, and individually
parts one of another. Having gifts that differ according to the
grace given to us, let us use them: if prophecy, in proportion to

our faith; if service, in our serving; the one who teaches, in teaching; [8]the one who exhorts, in exhortation; the one who contributes, in liberality; the one who gives aid, with zeal; the one who does acts of mercy, with cheerfulness.

GOSPEL

R E   Matthew 16:21–27
    L   Matthew 16:21–26

[21]From that time Jesus began to show his disciples that he must go to Jerusalem and suffer many things from the elders and the chief priests and scribes, and be killed, and on the third day be raised. And Peter took Jesus and began to rebuke him, saying, "God forbid, Lord! This shall never happen to you." But Jesus turned and said to Peter, "Get behind me, Satan! You are a hindrance to me; for you are thinking in human terms, and not in those of God."

Then Jesus told his disciples, "Those who would come after me, let them deny themselves and take up their cross and follow me. For those who would save their life will lose it, and those who would lose their life for my sake will find it. [26]For what do they profit, if they gain the whole world and forfeit their life? Or what shall they give in return for their life? [27]For the Man of Heaven is to come in the glory of his Father with his angels, and then will repay all according to their deeds."

R   TWENTY-SECOND SUNDAY IN ORDINARY TIME   **209**
E   PROPER 17
L   FIFTEENTH SUNDAY AFTER PENTECOST

R   TWENTY-THIRD SUNDAY IN ORDINARY TIME

E   PROPER 18

L   SIXTEENTH SUNDAY AFTER PENTECOST

FIRST READING

R L   Ezekiel 33:7–9

E   Ezekiel 33:7–11

7"You, O human one, I have made a sentry for the house of Israel; whenever you hear a word from my mouth, you shall give them warning from me. If I say to the wicked, O wicked ones, you shall surely die, and you do not speak to warn the wicked to turn from their way, those wicked ones shall die in their iniquity, but their blood I will require at your hand. 9But if you warn the wicked to turn from their way, and they do not turn from their way; they shall die in their iniquity, but you will have saved your life.

10"And you, O human one, say to the house of Israel, Thus have you said: 'Our transgressions and our sins are upon us, and we waste away because of them; how then can we live?' 11Say to them, As I live, says the Lord GOD, I have no pleasure in the death of the wicked, but that the wicked turn from their way and live; turn back, turn back from your evil ways; for why will you die, O house of Israel?"

SECOND READING

R   Romans 13:8–10

L   Romans 13:1–10

1Let every person be subject to the governing authorities. For there is no authority except from God, and those that exist have been instituted by God. Therefore the one who resists authorities resists what God has appointed, and those who resist will incur judgment. For rulers are not a terror to good conduct, but to bad. Would you have no fear of the one who is in authority? Then do what is good, and you will receive the approval of the authority who is God's servant for your good. But if you do wrong, be afraid, for the authority does not bear the sword in vain, but is the servant of God to execute God's wrath on the wrongdoer. Therefore one must be subject, not only to avoid God's wrath but also for the sake of conscience. For the same reason you also pay taxes, for the authorities are ministers of God, attending to this very thing. Pay all of them their dues, taxes to whom taxes are due, revenue to whom revenue is due, respect to whom respect is due, honor to whom honor is due.

⁸Owe no one anything, except to love one another; for they who love their neighbor have fulfilled the law. The commandments, "You shall not commit adultery, You shall not kill, You shall not steal, You shall not covet," and any other commandment, are summed up in this sentence, "You shall love your neighbor as yourself." ¹⁰Love does no wrong to a neighbor; therefore love is the fulfilling of the law.

E   Romans 12:9–21

⁹Let love be genuine; hate what is evil, hold fast to what is good; love one another with familial affection; outdo one another in showing honor. Never flag in zeal, be aglow with the Spirit, serve the Lord. Rejoice in your hope, be patient in tribulation, be constant in prayer. Contribute to the needs of the saints, practice hospitality.

Bless those who persecute you; bless and do not curse them. Rejoice with those who rejoice, weep with those who weep. Live in harmony with one another; do not be haughty, but associate with the lowly; never be conceited. Repay no one evil for evil, but take thought for what is noble in the sight of all. If possible, so far as it depends upon you, live peaceably with all. Beloved, never avenge yourselves, but leave it to the wrath of God; for it is written, "Vengeance is mine, I will repay, says the Lord." No, "if your enemies hunger, feed them; if they are thirsty, give them drink; for by so doing you will heap burning coals upon their head." ²¹Do not be overcome by evil, but overcome evil with good.

GOSPEL

R E L Matthew 18:15–20

[At that time Jesus said,]

15"If one of the community sins against you, go and reprove that person in private. If you are listened to, you have gained a friend. But if you are not listened to, take one or two others along with you, that every word may be confirmed by the evidence of two or three witnesses. If the offender refuses to listen to them, tell it to the church; and if the offender refuses to listen even to the church, let the offender be to you as a Gentile and a tax collector. Truly, I say to you, whatever you bind on earth shall be bound in heaven, and whatever you loose on earth shall be loosed in heaven. Again I say to you, if two of you agree on earth about anything they ask, it will be done for them by my Father in heaven. 20For where two or three are gathered in my name, there am I in the midst of them."

FIRST READING

R E Sirach 27:30–28:7

30Anger and wrath, these also are abominations,
  and the sinful will possess them.
They who take vengeance will suffer vengeance from the Lord,
  who will firmly establish their sins.
Forgive your neighbor the wrong which has been done,
  and then your sins will be pardoned when you pray.
Does one person harbor anger against another,
  and yet seek healing from the Lord?
Do people have no mercy toward others like themselves,
  and yet pray for their own sins?
If they themselves, being flesh, maintain wrath,
  who will make expiation for their sins?
Remember the end of your life, and cease from enmity,
  remember destruction and death, and be true to the
    commandments.
7Remember the commandments, and do not be angry with
    your neighbor;
  remember the covenant of the Most High, and overlook
    ignorance.

L Genesis 50:15–21

15When Joseph's brothers saw that their father was dead, they
said, "It may be that Joseph will hate us and pay us back for all
the evil which we did to him." So they sent a message to Joseph, saying, "Your father gave this command before he died,
'Say to Joseph, Forgive, I pray you, the transgression of your
brothers and their sin, because they did evil to you.' And now,
we pray you, forgive the transgressions of the servants of the
God of your father." Joseph wept when they spoke to him. His
brothers also came and fell down before him, and said, "Behold, we are your servants." But Joseph said to them, "Fear
not, for am I in the place of God? As for you, you meant evil

against me; but God meant it for good, to bring it about that many people should be kept alive, as they are today. ²¹So do not fear; I will provide for you and your little ones." Thus Joseph reassured them and comforted them.

SECOND READING

R   Romans 14:7–9
E   Romans 14:5–12
L   Romans 14:5–9

⁵One person esteems one day as better than another, while another esteems all days alike. Let all be fully convinced in their own mind. The one who observes the day, observes it in honor of the Lord. The one also who eats, eats in honor of the Lord, in giving thanks to God; while the one who abstains, abstains in honor of the Lord and gives thanks to God. ⁷We do not live to ourselves, and we do not die to ourselves. If we live, we live to the Lord, and if we die, we die to the Lord; so then, whether we live or whether we die, we are the Lord's. ⁹For to this end Christ died and lived again, that he might be Lord both of the dead and of the living.

¹⁰Why do you judge or denounce another person of the community? For we shall all stand before the judgment seat of God; for it is written,

"As I live, says the Lord, every knee shall bow to me,
and every tongue shall give praise to God."

¹²So we all shall give account of ourselves to God.

GOSPEL

R   E   L   Matthew 18:21–35

²¹Then Peter came up and said to Jesus, "Lord, how often shall someone sin against me, and I forgive? As many as seven times?" Jesus said to him, "I do not say to you seven times, but seventy times seven.

"Therefore the dominion of heaven may be compared to a king who wished to settle accounts with his servants. When he began the reckoning, one was brought to him who owed him ten

214   TWENTY-FOURTH SUNDAY IN ORDINARY TIME   R
       PROPER 19   E
       SEVENTEENTH SUNDAY OF PENTECOST   L

thousand talents; and as he could not pay, his lord ordered
him to be sold, with his wife and children and all that he had,
and payment to be made. So the servant fell on his knees, im-
ploring him, 'Lord, have patience with me, and I will pay you
everything.' And out of the pity for him the lord of that servant
released him and forgave him the debt. But that same servant,
as he went out, came upon another servant who owed him a
hundred denarii; and seizing him by the throat he said, 'Pay
what you owe.' So the servant fell down and besought him,
'Have patience with me, and I will pay you.' He refused and
went and put him in prison till he should pay the debt. When
the other servants saw what had taken place, they were greatly
distressed, and they went and reported to their lord all that
had taken place. Then his lord summoned him and said to
him, 'You wicked servant! I forgave you all that debt because
you besought me; and should not you have had mercy on the
other servant, as I had mercy on you?' And in anger his lord
delivered him to the jailers, till he should pay all his debt. [35]So
also my heavenly Father will do to every one of you, if you do
not forgive one another from your heart."

R TWENTY-FIFTH SUNDAY IN ORDINARY TIME
E PROPER 20
L EIGHTEENTH SUNDAY AFTER PENTECOST

FIRST READING

R L   Isaiah 55:6–9

⁶"Seek the Lord while the Lord may be found,
  call upon God, while God is near.
let the wicked forsake their ways
  and the unrighteous their thoughts;
let them return to the Lord, who will have mercy on them,
  and to our God, who will abundantly pardon.
For my thoughts are not your thoughts,
  neither are your ways my ways, says the Lord.
⁹For as the heavens are higher than the earth,
  so are my ways higher than your ways
  and my thoughts than your thoughts."

E   Jonah 3:10–4:11

¹⁰When God saw what the Ninevites did, how they turned
from their evil way, God repented of the evil which God had
said would be done to them; and God did not do it.

But it displeased Jonah exceedingly, and he was angry. And he
prayed to the Lord and said, "I pray you, Lord, is not this
what I said when I was yet in my country? That is why I made
haste to flee to Tarshish; for I knew that you are a gracious
God and merciful, slow to anger, and abounding in steadfast
love, and repent of evil. Therefore, now, O Lord, take my life
from me, I beseech you, for it is better for me to die than to
live." And the Lord said, "Do you do well to be angry?" Then
Jonah went out of the city and sat to the east of the city, and
made a booth for himself there. He sat under it in the shade,
till he should see what would become of the city.

And the Lord God appointed a plant, and made it come up
over Jonah, that it might be a shade over his head, to save him
from his discomfort. So Jonah was exceedingly glad because
of the plant. But when dawn came up the next day, God appointed a worm which attacked the plant, so that it withered.

When the sun rose, God appointed a sultry east wind, and the sun beat upon the head of Jonah so that he was faint; and he asked that he might die, and said, "It is better for me to die than to live." But God said to Jonah, "Do you do well to be angry for the plant?" And he said, "I do well to be angry, angry enough to die." And the LORD said, "You pity the plant, for which you did not labor, nor did you make it grow, which came into being in a night, and perished in a night. ¹¹And should not I pity Nineveh, that great city, in which there are more than a hundred and twenty thousand persons who do not know their right hand from their left, and also much cattle?"

SECOND READING

R   Philippians 1:20c–24, 27a
E   Philippians 1:21–27
L   Philippians 1:1–5, 19–27

¹Paul and Timothy, servants of Christ Jesus,

To all the saints in Christ Jesus who are at Philippi, with the bishops and deacons:

Grace to you and peace from God, our Father, and the Lord Jesus Christ.

I thank my God in all my remembrance of you, always in every prayer of mine for you all making my prayer with joy, ⁵thankful for your partnership in the gospel from the first day until now.

¹⁹Yes, and I shall rejoice. For I know that through your prayers and the help of the Spirit of Jesus Christ this will turn out for my deliverance, as it is my eager expectation and hope that I shall not be at all ashamed, but that with full courage now as always Christ will be honored in my body, ²⁰ᶜwhether by life or by death. ²¹For me to live is Christ, and to die is gain. If it is to be life in the flesh, that means fruitful labor for me. Yet which I shall choose I cannot tell. I am hard pressed between the two. My desire is to depart and be with Christ, for that is far better. ²⁴But to remain in the flesh is more necessary on your account. ²⁵Convinced of this, I know that I shall remain and continue

with you all, for your progress and joy in the faith, so that in me you may have ample cause to glory in Christ Jesus, because of my coming to you again.

27aOnly let your manner of life be worthy of the gospel of Christ, 27bso that whether I come and see you or am absent, I may hear of you that you stand firm in one spirit, with one mind striving side by side for the faith of the gospel.

GOSPEL

R E L   Matthew 20:1–16

[At that time Jesus said,]

1"For the dominion of heaven is like a householder who went out early in the morning to hire laborers for his vineyard. After agreeing with the laborers for a denarius a day, he sent them into his vineyard. And going out about the third hour he saw others standing idle in the market place; and to them he said, 'You go into the vineyard too, and whatever is right I will give you.' So they went. Going out again about the sixth hour and the ninth hour, he did the same. And about the eleventh hour he went out and found others standing; and he said to them, 'Why do you stand here idle all day?' They said to him, 'Because no one has hired us.' He said to them, 'You go into the vineyard too.' And when evening came, the owner of the vineyard said to his steward, 'Call the laborers and pay them their wages, beginning with the last, up to the first.' And when those hired about the eleventh hour came, each of them received a denarius. Now when the first came, they thought they would receive more; but each of them also received a denarius. And on receiving it they grumbled at the householder, saying, 'These last worked only one hour, and you have made them equal to us who have borne the burden of the day and the scorching heat.' But he replied to one of them, 'Friend, I am doing you no wrong; did you not agree with me for a denarius? Take what belongs to you, and go; I choose to give to this last as I give to you. Am I not allowed to do what I choose with what belongs to me? Or do you begrudge my generosity? 16So the last will be first, and the first last."

FIRST READING

R Ezekiel 18:25–28
E L Ezekiel 18:1–4, 25–32

¹The word of the LORD came to me again: "What do you mean by repeating this proverb concerning the land of Israel, 'The fathers have eaten sour grapes, and the children's teeth are set on edge'? As I live, says the Lord GOD, this proverb shall no more be used by you in Israel. ⁴Behold, all souls are mine; the soul of the father as well as the soul of the child is mine: the soul that sins shall die.

²⁵"Yet you say, 'The way of the Lord is not just.' Hear now, O house of Israel: Is my way not just? Is it not your ways that are not just? When the righteous turn away from their righteousness and commit iniquity, they shall die for it; for the iniquity which they have committed they shall die. Again, when the wicked turn away from the wickedness they have committed and do what is lawful and right, they shall save their life. ²⁸Because they considered and turned away from all the transgressions which they had committed, they shall surely live, they shall not die. ²⁹Yet the house of Israel says, 'The way of the Lord is not just.' O house of Israel, are my ways not just? Is it not your ways that are not just?

"Therefore I will judge you, O house of Israel, all of you according to your ways, says the Lord GOD. Repent and turn from all your transgressions, lest iniquity be your ruin. Cast away from you all the transgressions which you have committed against me, and get yourselves a new heart and a new spirit! Why will you die, O house of Israel? ³²For I have no pleasure in the death of any one, says the Lord GOD; so turn, and live."

SECOND READING

R   Philippians 2:1–11
E   Philippians 2:1–13
L   Philippians 2:1–5

¹So if there is any encouragement in Christ, any incentive of love, any participation in the Spirit, any affection and sympathy, complete my joy by being of the same mind, having the same love, being in full accord and of one mind. Do nothing from selfishness or conceit, but in humility count others better than yourselves. Let each of you look not only to your own interests, but also to the interests of others.

⁵Have this mind among yourselves, which is yours in Christ Jesus, ⁶who, being in the form of God, did not count equality with God a thing to be grasped, but gave it up, taking the form of a servant, being born in human likeness. And being found in human form he humbled himself and became obedient unto death, even death on a cross. Therefore God has highly exalted him and bestowed on him the name which is above every name, that at the name of Jesus every knee should bow, in heaven and on earth and under the earth, ¹¹and every tongue confess that Jesus Christ is Lord, to the glory of God, the Father.

¹²Therefore, my beloved, as you have always obeyed, so now, not only as in my presence but much more in my absence, work out your own salvation with fear and trembling; ¹³for God is at work in you, both to will and to work according to the divine good pleasure.

GOSPEL

R   E   L   Matthew 21:28–32

[At that time Jesus said,]

²⁸"What do you think? There was a man with two children who went to the first and said, 'Child, go and work in the vineyard today.' And he answered, 'I will not'; but afterward he repented and went. And he went to the second and said the same; and he answered, "I go, sir,' but did not go. Which of

the two did the will of the father?" They said, "The first." Jesus said to them, "Truly, I say to you, the tax collectors and the harlots go into the dominion of God before you. [32]For John came to you in the way of righteousness, and you did not believe him, but the tax collectors and the harlots believed him; and even when you saw it, you did not afterward repent and believe him."

R TWENTY-SEVENTH SUNDAY IN ORDINARY TIME
E PROPER 22
L TWENTIETH SUNDAY AFTER PENTECOST

FIRST READING

R E L Isaiah 5:1–7

¹Let me sing for the one I love
   a love song concerning my beloved's vineyard:
My beloved had a vineyard
   on a very fertile hill.
He digged it and cleared it of stones,
   and planted it with choice vines,
and built a watchtower in the midst of it,
   and hewed out a wine vat in it,
and looked for it to yield grapes,
   but it yielded wild grapes.
And now, O inhabitants of Jerusalem,
   and people of Judah,
judge, I pray you, between me
   and my vineyard.
What more was there to do for my vineyard,
   that I have not done in it?
When I look for it to yield grapes,
   why did it yield wild grapes?
And now I will tell you
   what I will do to my vineyard.
I will remove its hedge,
   and it shall be devoured;
I will break down its wall,
   and it shall be trampled down.
I will make it a waste;
   it shall not be pruned or hoed,
   and briars and thorns shall grow up;
I will also command the clouds
   that they rain no rain upon it.
⁷For the vineyard of the Lord of hosts
   is the house of Judah,

222 TWENTY-SEVENTH SUNDAY IN ORDINARY TIME   R
PROPER 22   E
TWENTIETH SUNDAY AFTER PENTECOST   L

and the people of Judah
  are God's pleasant planting;
and the LORD looked for justice,
  but behold, bloodshed;
for righteousness,
  but behold, a cry!

SECOND READING

R   Philippians 4:6–9

⁶Have no anxiety about anything; but in everything by prayer
and supplication with thanksgiving let your requests be made
known to God. And the peace of God, which passes all understanding, will keep your hearts and your minds in Christ Jesus.

Finally, my dear people, whatever is true, whatever is honorable, whatever is just, whatever is pure, whatever is lovely,
whatever is gracious, if there is any excellence, if there is anything worthy of praise, think about these things. ⁹What you
have learned and received and heard and seen in me, do; and
the God of peace will be with you.

E   Philippians 3:14–21
L   Philippians 3:12–21

¹²Not that I have already obtained this or am already perfect;
but I press on to make it my own, because Christ Jesus has
made me his own. My dear people, I do not consider that I
have made it my own; but one thing I do, forgetting what lies
behind and straining forward to what lies ahead, ¹⁴I press on
toward the goal for the prize of the upward call of God in
Christ Jesus. Let those of us who are mature be thus minded;
and if in anything you are otherwise minded, God will reveal
that also to you. Only let us hold true what we have attained.

My dear ones, join in imitating me, and mark those who so live
as you have an example in us. For many, of whom I have often
told you and now tell you even with tears, live as enemies of
the cross of Christ. Their end is destruction, their god is the
belly, and they glory in their shame, with minds set on earthly
things. But our commonwealth is in heaven, and from it we
await a Savior, the Lord Jesus Christ, ²¹who will change our

lowly body to be like his glorious body, by the power which enables him even to the subjection of all things.

GOSPEL

R   E   L   Matthew 21:33–43

[At that time Jesus said,]

33"Hear another parable. There was a householder who planted a vineyard, and set a hedge around it, and dug a wine press in it, and built a tower, and let it out to tenants, and went into another country. When the season of fruit drew near, the householder sent his servants to the tenants, to get his fruit; and the tenants took his servants and beat one, killed another, and stoned another. Again the householder sent other servants, more than the first; and they did the same to them. Afterward he sent his son to them, saying, 'They will respect my son.' But when the tenants saw the son, they said to themselves, 'This is the heir; come, let us kill him and have his inheritance.' And they took him and cast him out of the vineyard, and killed him. When therefore the owner of the vineyard comes, what will he do to those tenants?" They said to Jesus, "The owner will put those wretches to a miserable death, and let out the vineyard to other tenants who will give him the fruits in their seasons."

Jesus said to them, "Have you never read in scriptures:

'The very stone which the builders rejected
has become the head of the corner;
this was the Lord's doing,
and it is marvelous in our eyes'?

43Therefore I tell you, the dominion of God will be taken away from you and given to a nation producing the fruits of it."

224   TWENTY-SEVENTH SUNDAY IN ORDINARY TIME   R
PROPER 22   E
TWENTIETH SUNDAY AFTER PENTECOST   L

R **TWENTY-EIGHTH SUNDAY IN ORDINARY TIME**
E **PROPER 23**
L **TWENTY-FIRST SUNDAY AFTER PENTECOST**

FIRST READING

R Isaiah 25:6–10a
E Isaiah 25:1–9
L Isaiah 25:6–9

¹O Lord, you are my God;
    I will exalt you, I will praise your name;
for you have done wonderful things,
    plans formed of old, faithful and sure.
For you have made the city a heap,
    the fortified city is a ruin;
the palace of aliens is a city no more,
    it will never be rebuilt.
Therefore strong peoples will glorify you;
    cities of ruthless nations will fear you.
For you have been a stronghold to the poor,
    a stronghold to the needy in their distress,
    a shelter from the storm and a shade from the heat;
for the blast of the ruthless is like a storm against a wall,
    like heat in a dry place.
You subdue the noise of the aliens;
    as heat by the shade of a cloud,
    so the song of the ruthless is stilled.

⁶On this mountain the Lord of hosts will make for all people a
feast of fat things, a feast of wine on the lees, of fat things full
of marrow, of wine on the lees well refined. And the Lord will
destroy on this mountain the covering that is cast over all
peoples, the veil that is spread over all nations. The Lord will
swallow up death for ever, and the Lord God will wipe away
tears from all faces, and the reproach of God's people the Lord
will take away from all the earth; for the Lord has spoken.

⁹It will be said on that day, "Lo, this is our God, for whom we
have waited, that God might save us. This is the Lord, for

whom we have waited; let us be glad and rejoice in the salvation of the LORD

10a"For the hand of the LORD will rest on this mountain."

SECOND READING

R Philippians 4:12–14, 19–20
E L Philippians 4:4–13

4Rejoice in the Lord always; again I will say, Rejoice. Let everyone know your forbearance. The Lord is at hand. Have no anxiety about anything; but in everything by prayer and supplication with thanksgiving let your requests be made known to God. And the peace of God, which passes all understanding, will keep your hearts and your minds in Christ Jesus.

Finally, my dear people, whatever is true, whatever is honorable, whatever is just, whatever is pure, whatever is lovely, whatever is gracious, if there is any excellence, if there is anything worthy of praise, think about these things. What you have learned and received and heard and seen in me, do; and the God of peace will be with you.

I rejoice in the Lord greatly that now at length you have revived your concern for me; you were indeed concerned for me, but you had no opportunity. Not that I complain of want; for I have learned, in whatever state I am, to be content. 12I know how to be abased, and I know how to abound; in any and all circumstances I have learned the secret of facing plenty and hunger, abundance and want. 13I can do all things in the one who strengthens me.

14Yet it was kind of you to share my trouble.

19And my God will supply every need of yours according to the divine riches in glory in Christ Jesus. 20To God, our Father, be glory for ever and ever. Amen.

GOSPEL

R E   Matthew 22:1–14
L   Matthew 22:1–10

¹Again Jesus spoke to them in parables, saying, "The dominion of heaven may be compared to a king who gave a marriage feast for his son, and sent his servants to call those who were invited to the marriage feast; but they would not come. Again he sent other servants, saying, 'Tell those who are invited, Behold, I have made ready my dinner, my oxen amd fat calves are killed, and everything is ready; come to the marriage feast.' But they made light of it and went off, one to a farm, another to business, while the rest seized his servants, treated them shamefully, and killed them. The king was angry, and he sent his troops and destroyed those murderers and burned their city. Then he said to his servants, 'The wedding is ready, but those invited were not worthy. Go therefore to the thoroughfares, and invite to the marriage feast as many as you find.' ¹⁰And those servants went out into the streets and gathered all whom they found, both bad and good; so the wedding hall was filled with guests.

¹¹"But when the king came in to look at the guests, he saw there a person who had no wedding garment; and he said to him, 'Friend, how did you get in here without a wedding garment?' And he was speechless. Then the king said to the attendants, 'Bind him hand and foot, and cast him into the outer darkness; there they will weep and gnash their teeth.' ¹⁴For many are called, but few are chosen."

R   TWENTY-EIGHTH SUNDAY IN ORDINARY TIME   227
E   PROPER 23
L   TWENTY-FIRST SUNDAY AFTER PENTECOST

R TWENTY-NINTH SUNDAY IN ORDINARY TIME
E PROPER 24
L TWENTY-SECOND SUNDAY AFTER PENTECOST

FIRST READING

R Isaiah 45:1, 4–6
E L Isaiah 45:1–7

¹Thus says the LORD to Cyrus, the LORD's anointed,
   whose right hand I have grasped,
to subdue nations before the LORD
   and to strip their rulers,
to open doors before Cyrus
   that gates may not be closed:
²"I will go before you
   and level the mountains,
I will break in pieces the doors of bronze
   and cut asunder the bars of iron,
I will give you the treasures of darkness
   and the hoards in secret places,
that you may know that it is I, the LORD,
   the God of Israel, who call you by your name.
⁴For the sake of my servant Jacob,
   and Israel my chosen,
I call you by your name,
   I surname you, though you do not know me.
I am the LORD, and there is no other,
   besides me there is no God;
   I gird you, though you do not know me,
⁶that everyone may know, from the rising of the sun
   and from the west, that there is none besides me;
   I am the LORD, and there is no other.
⁷I form the light and create darkness,
   I make weal and create woe,
   I am the LORD, who do all these things."

SECOND READING

R L   1 Thessalonians 1:1–5a
   E   1 Thessalonians 1:1–10

¹Paul, Silvanus, and Timothy,

To the church of the Thessalonians in God, the Father, and the Lord Jesus Christ:

Grace to you and peace.

We give thanks to God always for you all, constantly mentioning you in our prayers, remembering before God, our Father, your work of faith and labor of love and steadfastness of hope in our Lord Jesus Christ. For we know, my dear people beloved by God, that God has chosen you; ⁵ᵃfor our gospel came to you not only in word, but also in power and in the Holy Spirit and with full conviction. ⁵ᵇYou know what sort of persons we proved to be among you for your sake. And you became imitators of us and of the Lord, for you received the word in much affliction, with joy inspired by the Holy Spirit; so that you became an example to all the believers in Macedonia and in Achaia. For not only has the word of the Lord sounded forth from you in Macedonia and Achaia, but your faith in God has gone forth everywhere, so that we need not say anything. For they themselves report concerning us what a welcome we had among you, and how you turned to God from idols, to serve a living and true God, ¹⁰and to wait for God's Son from heaven, whom God raised from the dead, Jesus who delivers us from the wrath to come.

GOSPEL

R L   Matthew 22:15–21
   E   Matthew 22:15–22

¹⁵The Pharisees went and took counsel how to entangle Jesus in his talk. And they sent their disciples to Jesus, along with the Herodians, saying, "Teacher, we know that you are true, and teach the way of God truthfully, and care about no one's opinion; for you are no respecter of persons. Tell us, then, what you think. Is it lawful to pay taxes to Caesar, or not?" But Je-

sus, aware of their malice, said, "Why put me to the test, you hypocrites? Show me the money for the tax." And they brought him a coin. And Jesus said to them, "Whose likeness and inscription is this?" [21]They said, "Caesar's." Then Jesus said to them, "Render therefore to Caesar the things that are Caesar's, and to God the things that are God's." [22]When they heard it, they marveled; and they left Jesus and went away.

R THIRTIETH SUNDAY IN ORDINARY TIME
E PROPER 25
L TWENTY-THIRD SUNDAY AFTER PENTECOST

FIRST READING

R Exodus 22:20–26
E Exodus 22:21–27

20/21"You shall not wrong or oppress a stranger, for you were strangers in the land of Egypt. You shall not afflict any widow or orphan. If you do afflict them, and they cry out to me, I will surely hear their cry; and my wrath will burn, and I will kill your men with the sword, and your wives shall become widows and your children fatherless.

"If you lend money to any of my people with you who is poor, you shall not present yourself as a creditor, and you shall not exact interest. If ever you take your neighbor's garment in pledge, you shall restore it before the sun goes down; 26/27for this mantle is the only body covering your neighbor has; in what else shall your neighbor sleep? And if this poor one cries to me, I will hear, for I am compassionate."

L Leviticus 19:1–2, 15–18

1The LORD said to Moses, 2"Say to all the congregation of the people of Israel, You shall be holy; for I the LORD your God am holy.

15"You shall do no injustice in judgment; you shall not be partial to the poor or defer to the great, but in righteousness shall you judge your neighbor. You shall not go up and down as a slanderer among your people, and you shall not stand forth against the life of your neighbor: I am the LORD.

"You shall not hate your neighbor in your heart, but you shall reason with your neighbor, lest you thereby bear sin. 18You shall not take vengeance or bear any grudge against your own people, but you shall love your neighbor as yourself: I am the LORD."

SECOND READING

R L 1 Thessalonians 1:5b–10

⁵ᵇYou know what sort of persons we proved to be among you for your sake. And you became imitators of us and of the Lord, for you received the word in much affliction, with joy inspired by the Holy Spirit; so that you became an example to all the believers in Macedonia and in Achaia. For not only has the word of the Lord sounded forth from you in Macedonia and Achaia, but your faith in God has gone forth everywhere, so that we need not say anything. For they themselves report concerning us what a welcome we had among you, and how you turned to God from idols, to serve a living and true God, ¹⁰and to wait for God's Son from heaven, whom God raised from the dead, Jesus who delivers us from the wrath to come.

E 1 Thessalonians 2:1–8

¹You yourselves know, my dear people, that our visit to you was not in vain; but though we had already suffered and been shamefully treated at Philippi, as you know, we had courage in our God to declare to you the gospel of God in the face of great opposition. For our appeal does not spring from error or uncleanness, nor is it made with guile; but just as we have been approved by God to be entrusted with the gospel, so we speak, not to please human beings, but to please God who tests our hearts. For we never used either words of flattery, as you know, or a cloak for greed, as God is witness; nor did we seek glory from human beings, whether from you or from others, though we might have made demands as apostles of Christ. But we were gentle among you, like a nursing mother taking care of her children. ⁸So, being affectionately desirous of you, we were ready to share with you not only the gospel of God but also our very own lives, because you had become very dear to us.

GOSPEL

R L   Matthew 22:34–40
  E   Matthew 22:34–46

[34]When the Pharisees heard that Jesus had silenced the Sadducees, they came together. And one of them, a lawyer, asked Jesus a question, to test him. "Teacher, which is the great commandment in the law?" And Jesus said to him, "You shall love the Lord your God with all your heart, and with all your soul, and with all your mind. This is the great and first commandment. And a second is like it, You shall love your neighbor as yourself. [40]On these two commandments depend all the law and the prophets."

[41]Now while the Pharisees were gathered together, Jesus asked them a question, saying, "What do you think of the Christ? Whose son is he?" They said to him, "The son of David." Jesus said to them, "How is it then that David, inspired by the Spirit, calls him Lord, saying,

'The Lord said to my Lord,
Sit at my right hand,
till I put your enemies under your feet'?

If David thus calls him Lord, how is he David's son?" [46]And no one was able to answer him a word, nor from that day did any one dare to ask him any more questions.

R **THIRTY-FIRST SUNDAY IN ORDINARY TIME**

E **PROPER 26**

L **TWENTY-FOURTH SUNDAY AFTER PENTECOST**

FIRST READING

R Malachi 1:14b–2:2b, 8–10

[14b]"I am a great Sovereign, says the LORD of hosts, and my name is feared among the nations.

"And now, O priests, this command is for you. [2a]If you will not listen, if you will not lay it to heart to give glory to my name, says the LORD of hosts,[2b] then I will send the curse upon you and I will curse your blessings. [8]But you have turned aside from the way; you have caused many to stumble by your instruction; you have corrupted the covenant of Levi, says the LORD of hosts, and so I make you despised and abased before all the people, inasmuch as you have not kept my ways but have shown partiality in your instruction."

[10]Is there not one father for our people? Has not one God created us? Why then are we faithless to one another, profaning the covenant of our forebears?

E Micah 3:5–12

[5]Thus says the LORD concerning the prophets
  who lead my people astray,
who cry "Peace"
  when they have something to eat,
but declare war against one
  who puts nothing into their mouths.
Therefore it shall be night to you, without vision,
  and darkness to you, without divination.
The sun shall go down upon the prophets,
  and the day shall be black over them;
the seers shall be disgraced,
  and the diviners put to shame;
they shall all cover their lips,
  for there is no answer from God.

But as for me, I am filled with power,
  with the Spirit of the LORD,
  and with justice and might,
to declare to Jacob its transgression
  and to Israel its sin.
Hear this, you heads of the house of Jacob
  and rulers of the house of Israel,
who abhor justice
  and pervert all equity,
who build Zion with blood
  and Jerusalem with wrong.
Its heads give judgment for a bribe,
  its priests teach for hire,
  its prophets divine for money;
yet they lean upon the LORD and say,
  "Is not the LORD in the midst of us?
  No evil shall come upon us."
[12]Therefore because of you
  Zion shall be plowed as a field;
Jerusalem shall become a heap of ruins,
  and the mountain of the house a wooded height.

L   Amos 5:18–24

[18]Woe to you who desire the day of the LORD!
  Why would you have the day of the LORD?
It is darkness, and not light;
  as if a man fled from a lion,
  and a bear met him;
or went into the house and leaned with his hand against the
    wall,
  and a serpent bit him.
Is not the day of the LORD darkness, and not light,
  and gloom with no brightness in it?
"I hate, I despise your feasts,
  and I take no delight in your solemn assemblies.
Even though you offer me your burnt offerings and cereal
    offerings,
  I will not accept them,

and the peace offerings of your fatted beasts
    I will not look upon.
Take away from me the noise of your songs;
    to the melody of your harps I will not listen.
²⁴But let justice roll down like waters,
    and righteousness like an ever-flowing stream."

SECOND READING

R   1 Thessalonians 2:7b–9, 13
E   1 Thessalonians 2:9–13, 17–20

⁷ᵇWe were gentle among you, like a nursing mother taking care of her children. So, being affectionately desirous of you, we were ready to share with you not only the gospel of God but also our own lives, because you had become very dear to us.

⁹For you remember our labor and toil, my dear people; we worked night and day, that we might not burden any of you, while we preached to you the gospel of God. ¹⁰You are witnesses, and God also, how holy and righteous and blameless was our behavior to you believers; for you know how, like a father with his children, we exhorted each one of you and encouraged you and charged you to lead a life worthy of God, who calls you into God's own dominion and glory.

¹³And we also thank God constantly for this, that when you received the word of God which you heard from us, you accepted it not as a human word but as what it really is, the word of God, which is at work in you believers.

¹⁷But since we were bereft of you, my dear ones, for a short time, in person not in heart, we endeavored the more eagerly and with great desire to see you face to face; because we wanted to come to you—I, Paul, again and again—but Satan hindered us. For what is our hope or joy or crown of boasting before our Lord Jesus at his coming? Is it not you? ²⁰For you are our glory and joy.

L   1 Thessalonians 4:13–14

¹³We would not have you ignorant, my dear people, concerning those who are asleep, that you may not grieve as others do who have no hope. ¹⁴For since we believe that Jesus died and

236   THIRTY-FIRST SUNDAY IN ORDINARY TIME   R
       PROPER 26   E
       TWENTY-FOURTH SUNDAY AFTER PENTECOST   L

rose again, even so, through Jesus, God will bring with him
those who have fallen asleep.

GOSPEL

R E   Matthew 23:1–12

¹Jesus said to the crowds and to his disciples, "The scribes and
the Pharisees sit on Moses' seat; so practice and observe whatever they tell you, but not what they do; for they preach, but
do not practice. They bind heavy burdens, hard to bear, and
lay them on the people's shoulders; but they themselves will
not move them with their finger. They do all their deeds to be
seen by others; for they make their phylacteries broad and their
fringes long, and they love the place of honor at feasts and the
best seats in the synagogues, and the salutations in the market
places, and being called rabbi by others. But you are not to be
called rabbi, for you have one teacher, and you are all compan-
ions. And call no one on earth your father, for you have One,
the Father in heaven. Neither be called instructor, for you have
one instructor, the Christ. The one greatest among you shall be
your servant; ¹²those who exalt themselves will be humbled,
and those who humble themselves will be exalted."

L   Matthew 25:1–13

[At that time Jesus said,]

¹"The dominion of heaven shall be compared to ten maidens
who took their lamps and went to meet the bridegroom. Five of
them were foolish, and five were wise. For when the foolish
took their lamps, they took no oil with them; but the wise took
flasks of oil with their lamps. As the bridegroom was delayed,
they all slumbered and slept. But at midnight there was a cry,
'Behold, the bridegroom! Come out to meet him.' Then all
those maidens rose and trimmed their lamps. And the foolish
said to the wise, "Give us some of your oil, for our lamps are
going out.' But the wise replied, 'Perhaps there will not be
enough for us and for you; go rather to the dealers and buy for
yourselves.' And while they went to buy, the bridegroom,
came and those who were ready went with him to the marriage
feast; and the door was shut. Afterward the other maidens

came also, saying, 'Sir, sir, open to us.' But he replied, 'Truly, I say to you, I do not know you.' [13]Watch therefore, for you know neither the day nor the hour."

R THIRTY-SECOND SUNDAY IN ORDINARY TIME
E PROPER 27
L TWENTY-FIFTH SUNDAY AFTER PENTECOST

FIRST READING

R   Wisdom 6:12–16

¹²Wisdom is radiant and unfading,
and she is easily discerned by those who love her,
and is found by those who seek her.
She hastens to make herself known to those who desire her.
He who rises early to seek her will have no difficulty,
for he will find her sitting at his gates.
To fix one's thought on her is perfect understanding,
and he who is vigilant on her account will soon be free from
        care,
¹⁶because she goes about seeking those worthy of her,
and she graciously appears to them in their paths,
and meets them in every thought.

E   Amos 5:18–24

¹⁸Woe to you who desire the day of the LORD!
    Why would you have the day of the LORD?
It is darkness, and not light;
    as if a man fled from a lion,
    and a bear met him;
or went into the house and leaned with his hand against the
        wall,
    and a serpent bit him.
Is not the day of the LORD darkness, and not light,
    and gloom with no brightness in it?
"I hate, I despise your feasts,
    and I take no delight in your solemn assemblies.
Even though you offer me your burnt offerings and cereal
        offerings,
    I will not accept them,
and the peace offerings of your fatted beasts
    I will not look upon.

Take away from me the noise of your songs;
  to the melody of your harps I will not listen.
²⁴But let justice roll down like waters,
  and righteousness like an ever-flowing stream."

L Hosea 11:1–4, 8–9

¹When Israel was a child, I loved him,
  and out of Egypt I called my son.
The more I called them,
  the more they went from me;
they kept sacrificing to the Baals,
  and burning incense to idols.
Yet it was I who taught Ephraim to walk,
  I took them up in my arms;
  but they did not know that I healed them.
⁴I led them with cords of compassion,
  with the bands of love,
and I became to them as one
  who eases the yoke on their jaws,
  and I bent down to them and fed them.
⁸How can I give you up, O Ephraim!
  How can I hand you over, O Israel!
How can I make you like Admah!
  How can I treat you like Zeboiim!
My heart recoils within me,
  my compassion grows warm and tender.
⁹I will not execute my fierce anger,
  I will not again destroy Ephraim;
for I am God and not a man,
  the Holy One in your midst,
  and I will not come to destroy.

SECOND READING

R E 1 Thessalonians 4:13–18

¹³We would not have you ignorant, my dear people, concerning
those who are asleep, that you may not grieve as others do
who have no hope. For since we believe that Jesus died and
rose again, even so, through Jesus, God will bring with him
those who have fallen asleep. For this we declare to you by the

word of the Lord, that we who are alive, who are left until the coming of the Lord, shall not precede those who have fallen asleep. For that very Lord will descend from heaven with a cry of command, with the archangel's call, and with the sound of the trumpet of God. And the dead in Christ will rise first; then we who are alive, who are left, shall be caught up together with them in the clouds to meet the Lord in the air; and so we shall always be with the Lord. [18]Therefore comfort one another with these words.

L 1 Thessalonians 5:1–11

[1]As to the times and the seasons, my dear people, you have no need to have anything written to you. For you yourselves know well that the day of the Lord will come like a thief in the night. When people say, "There is peace and security," then sudden destruction will come upon them as labor pangs come upon a woman with child, and there will be no escape. But you are not in darkness, my dear people, for that day to surprise you like a thief. For you are all children of light and children of the day; we are not of the night or of darkness. So then let us not sleep, as others do, but let us keep awake and be sober. For those who sleep sleep at night, and those who get drunk are drunk at night. But, since we belong to the day, let us be sober, and put on the breastplate of faith and love, and for a helmet the hope of salvation. For God has not destined us for wrath, but to obtain salvation through our Lord Jesus Christ, who died for us so that whether we wake or sleep we might live with him. [11]Therefore encourage one another and build one another up, just as you are doing.

GOSPEL

R E Matthew 25:1–13

[At that time Jesus said,]

[1]"The dominion of heaven shall be compared to ten maidens who took their lamps and went to meet the bridegroom. Five of them were foolish, and five were wise. For when the foolish took their lamps, they took no oil with them; but the wise took flasks of oil with their lamps. As the bridegroom was delayed,

they all slumbered and slept. But at midnight there was a cry, 'Behold, the bridegroom! Come out to meet him.' Then all those maidens rose and trimmed their lamps. And the foolish said to the wise, 'Give us some of your oil, for our lamps are going out.' But the wise replied, 'Perhaps there will not be enough for us and for you; go rather to the dealers and buy for yourselves.' And while they went to buy, the bridegroom came, and those who were ready went in with him to the marriage feast; and the door was shut. Afterward the other maidens came also, saying, 'Sir, sir, open to us,' but he replied, 'Truly, I say to you, I do not know you.' [13]Watch therefore, for you know neither the day nor the hour."

L   Matthew 25:14–30

[At that time Jesus said,]

[14]"It will be as when a person going on a journey called his slaves and entrusted to them his property; to one he gave five talents, to another two, to another one, each according to his ability. Then he went away. The one who had received the five talents went at once and traded with them and made five talents more. So also, the one who had the two talents made two talents more. But the one who had received the single talent went and dug in the ground and hid his master's money. Now after a long time the master of those slaves came and settled accounts with them. And the one who had received the five talents came forward, bringing five talents more, saying, 'Master, you delivered to me five talents; here I have made five talents more.' His master said to him, 'Well done, good and faithful slave, you have been faithful over a little, I will set you over much; enter into the joy of your master.' And the one also who had the two talents came forward, saying, 'Master, you delivered to me two talents; here I have made two talents more.' His master said to him, 'Well done, good and faithful slave, you have been faithful over a little, I will set you over much; enter into the joy of your master." The one also who had received the single talent came forward, saying, 'Master, I know you to be a hard man, reaping where you did not sow, and gathering where you did not winnow; so I was afraid, and I went and hid your talent in the ground. Here you have what

is yours.' But his master answered him, 'You wicked and sloth-ful slave! You knew that I reap where I have not sowed, and gather where I have not winnowed? Then you ought to have invested my money with bankers, and at my coming I should have received what was my own with interest. So take the tal-ent from him, and give it to the one who has the ten talents. For to every one who has will more be given, unto abundnce; but from one who has not, even that little will be taken away. 30And cast the worthless slave into the outer darkness, where there shall be weeping and gnashing of teeth.' "

R   THIRTY-THIRD SUNDAY IN ORDINARY TIME
E   PROPER 28
L   TWENTY-SIXTH SUNDAY AFTER PENTECOST

FIRST READING

R   Proverbs 31:10–13, 19–20, 30–31   §

¹⁰A good wife who can find?
    She is far more precious than jewels.
The heart of her husband trusts in her,
    and he will have no lack of gain.
She does him good, and not harm,
    all the days of her life.
¹³She seeks wool and flax,
    and works with willing hands.
¹⁹She puts her hands to the distaff,
    and her hands hold the spindle.
²⁰She opens her hand to the poor,
    and reaches out her hand to the needy.
³⁰Charm is deceitful, and beauty is vain,
    but a woman who fears the LORD is to be praised.
³¹Give her of the fruit of her hands,
    and let her works praise her in the gates.

E   Zephaniah 1:7, 12–18

⁷Be silent before the Lord GOD!
    For the day of the LORD is at hand;
the LORD has prepared a sacrifice
    and consecrated those who are called.
¹²"At that time," says the LORD, "I will search Jerusalem with
    lamps,
    and I will punish those
who are thickening upon their lees,
    those who say in their hearts,
'The LORD will not do good,
    nor will the LORD do ill.'
Their goods shall be plundered,
    and their houses laid waste.
Though they build houses,
    they shall not inhabit them;

though they plant vineyards,
    they shall not drink wine from them."
The great day of the Lord is near,
    near and hastening fast;
the sound of the day of the Lord is bitter,
    the mighty soldier cries aloud there.
A day of wrath is that day,
    a day of distress and anguish,
a day of ruin and devastation,
    a day of darkness and gloom,
a day of clouds and thick darkness,
    a day of trumpet blast and battle cry
against the fortified cities
    and against the lofty battlements.
So I will bring distress on humankind,
    so that they shall walk like the blind,
    because they have sinned against the Lord;
their blood shall be poured out like dust,
    and their flesh like dung.
[18]Neither their silver nor their gold
    shall be able to deliver them
    on the day of the wrath of the Lord.
In the fire of the Lord's jealous wrath,
    all the earth shall be consumed;
for a full, yes, sudden end
    the Lord will make of all the inhabitants of the earth.

L   Malachi 2:1–2, 4–10

[1]"And now, O priests, this command is for you. [2]If you will not listen, if you will not lay it to heart to give glory to my name, says the Lord of hosts, then I will send the curse upon you and I will curse your blessings; indeed I have already cursed them, because you do not lay it to heart. [4]So shall you know that I have sent this command to you, that my covenant with Levi may hold, says the Lord of hosts. My covenant with Levi was a covenant of life and peace, and I gave them to him, that he might fear; and he feared me, he stood in awe of my name. True instruction was in his mouth, and no wrong was found on his lips. He walked with me in peace and upright-

R   THIRTY-THIRD SUNDAY IN ORDINARY TIME 245
E   PROPER 28
L   TWENTY-SIXTH SUNDAY AFTER PENTECOST

ness, and he turned many from iniquity. For the lips of a priest should guard knowledge, and people should seek instruction from his mouth, for he is the messenger of the LORD of hosts. But you have turned aside from the way; you have caused many to stumble by your instruction; you have corrupted the covenant of Levi, says the LORD of hosts, and so I make you despised and abased before all the people, inasmuch as you have not kept my ways but have shown partiality in your instruction."

¹⁰Is there not one father for our people? Has not one God created us? Why then are we faithless to one another, profaning the covenant of our forebears?

SECOND READING

R 1 Thessalonians 5:1–6
E 1 Thessalonians 5:1–10

¹As to the times and the seasons, my dear people, you have no need to have anything written to you. For you yourselves know well that the day of the Lord will come like a thief in the night. When people say, "There is peace and security," then sudden destruction will come upon them as labor pangs come upon a woman with child, and there will be no escape. But you are not in darkness, my dear people, for that day to surprise you like a thief. For you are all children of light and children of the day; we are not of the night or of darkness. ⁶So then let us not sleep, as others do, but let us keep awake and be sober. ⁷For those who sleep sleep at night, and those who get drunk are drunk at night. But, since we belong to the day, let us be sober, and put on the breastplate of faith and love, and for a helmet the hope of salvation. For God has not destined us for wrath, but to obtain salvation through our Lord Jesus Christ, ¹⁰who died for us so that whether we wake or sleep we might live with him.

L 1 Thessalonians 2:8–13

⁸Being affectionately desirous of you, we were ready to share with you not only the gospel of God but also our own lives, because you had become very dear to us.

For you remember our labor and toil, my dear people; we worked night and day, that we might not burden any of you, while we preached to you the gospel of God. You are witnesses, and God also, how holy and righteous and blameless was our behavior to you believers; for you know how, like a father with his children, we exhorted each one of you and encouraged you and charged you to lead a life worthy of God, who calls you into God's own dominion and glory.

¹³And we also thank God constantly for this, that when you received the word of God which you heard from us, you accepted it not as a human word but as what it really is, the word of God, which is at work in you believers.

GOSPEL

R   Matthew 25:14–30
E   Matthew 25:14–15, 19–29

[At that time Jesus said,]

¹⁴"It will be as when a person going on a journey called his slaves and entrusted to them his property; ¹⁵to one he gave five talents, to another two, to another one, to each according to his ability. Then he went away. ¹⁶The one who had received the five talents went out at once and traded with them and made five talents more. So also, the one who had received the two talents made two talents more. But the one who had received the single talent went and dug in the ground and hid his master's money. ¹⁹Now after a long time the master of those slaves came and settled accounts with them. And the one who had received the five talents came forward, bringing five talents more, saying, 'Master, you delivered to me five talents; here I have made five talents more.' His master said to him, 'Well done, good and faithful slave, you have been faithful over a little, I will set you over much; enter into the joy of your master.' And the one also who had two talents came forward, saying, 'Master, you delivered to me two talents; here I have made two talents more.' His master said to him, 'Well done, good and faithful slave, you have been faithful over a little, I will set you over much; enter into the joy of your master." The

one also who had received the single talent came forward, saying, 'Master, I know you to be a hard man, reaping where you
did not sow, and gathering where you did not winnow; so I
was afraid, and I went and hid your talent in the ground. Here
you have what is yours.' But his master answered him, 'You
wicked and slothful slave! You knew that I reap where I have
not sowed, and gather where I have not winnowed? Then you
ought to have invested my money with the bankers, and at my
coming I should have received what was my own with interest.
So take the talent from him, and give it to the one who has the
ten talents. ²⁹For to every one who has will more be given,
unto abundance; but from one who has not, even that little will
be taken away. ³⁰And cast the worthless slave into the outer
darkness, where there shall be weeping and gnashing of
teeth.' "

L   Matthew 23:1–12
                        1
¹Jesus said to the crowds and to his disciples, "The scribes and
the Pharisees sit on Moses' seat; so practice and observe whatever they tell you, but not what they do; for they preach, but
do not practice. They bind heavy burdens, hard to bear, and
lay them on the people's shoulders; but they themselves will
not move them with their finger. They do all their deeds to be
seen by others; for they make their phylacteries broad and their
fringes long, and they love the place of honor at feasts and the
best seats in the synagogues, and salutations in the market
places, and being called rabbi by others. But you are not to be
called rabbi, for you have one teacher, and you are all compan-
ions. And call no one on earth your father, for you have One,
the Father in heaven. Neither be called instructor, for you have
one instructor, the Christ. The one who is greatest among you
shall be your servant; ¹²those who exalt themselves will be
humbled, and those who humble themselves will be exalted."

L TWENTY-SEVENTH SUNDAY AFTER PENTECOST

FIRST READING

L Jeremiah 26:1–6

¹In the beginning of the reign of Jehoiakim the son of Josiah, king of Judah, this word came from the LORD, "Thus says the LORD: Stand in the court of the LORD's house, and speak to all the cities of Judah which come to worship in the house of the LORD all the words that I command you to speak to them; do not hold back a word. It may be they will listen, and all turn from their evil ways, that I may repent of the evil which I intend to do to them because of their evil doings. You shall say to them, 'Thus says the LORD: If you will not listen to me, to walk in my law which I have set before you, and to heed the words of my servants the prophets whom I send to you urgently, though you have not heeded, ⁶then I will make this house like Shiloh, and I will make this city a curse for all the nations of the earth.'"

SECOND READING

L 1 Thessalonians 3:7–13

⁷For this reason, my dear people, in all our distress and affliction we have been comforted about you through your faith; for now we live, if you stand fast in the Lord. For what thanksgiving can we render to God for you, for all the joy which we feel for your sake before God, praying earnestly night and day that we may see you face to face and supply what is lacking in your faith?

Now may that very God, our Father, and our Lord Jesus, direct our way to you; and may the Lord make you increase and abound in love to one another and to all, as we do to you, ¹³to establish your hearts unblamable in the holiness before God, our Father, at the coming of our Lord Jesus with all his saints.

GOSPEL

L   Matthew 24:1–14

¹Jesus left the temple and was going away, when his disciples came to point out to him the buildings of the temple. But he answered them, "You see all these, do you not? Truly, I say to you, there will not be left here one stone upon another, that will not be thrown down."

As Jesus sat on the Mount of Olives, the disciples came to him privately, saying, "Tell us, when will this be, and what will be the sign of your coming and of the close of the age?" And Jesus answered them, "Take heed that no one leads you astray. For many will come in my name, saying, 'I am the Christ,' and they will lead many astray. And you will hear of wars and rumors of wars; see that you are not alarmed; for this must take place, but the end is not yet. For nation will rise against nation, and country against country, and there will be famines and earthquakes in various places: all this but the beginning of the birth-pangs.

"Then they will deliver you up to tribulation, and put you to death; and you will be hated by all nations for my name's sake. And then many will fall away, and betray one another, and hate one another. And many false prophets will arise and lead many astray. And because wickedness is multiplied, the love of many will grow cold. But the one who endures to the end will be saved. ¹⁴And this gospel of God's dominion will be preached throughout the whole world, as a testimony to all nations; and then the end will come."

R THIRTY-FOURTH OR LAST SUNDAY OF THE YEAR, CHRIST THE KING
E PROPER 29
L CHRIST THE KING

FIRST READING

R Ezekiel 34:11–12, 15–17
E Ezekiel 34:11–17
L Ezekiel 34:11–16, 23–24

[11]"For thus says the Lord GOD: Behold, I, I myself will search for my sheep, and will seek them out. [12]As a shepherd seeks out the flock when some of the sheep have been scattered abroad, so will I seek out my sheep; and I will rescue them from all places where they have been scattered on a day of clouds and thick darkness. [13]And I will bring them out from the peoples, and gather them from the countries, and will bring them into their own land; and I will feed them on the mountains of Israel, by the fountains, and in all the inhabited places of the country. I will feed them with good pasture, and upon the mountain heights of Israel shall be their pasture; there they shall lie down in good grazing land, and on fat pasture they shall feed on the mountains of Israel. [15]I myself will be the shepherd of my sheep, and I will make them lie down, says the Lord GOD. [16]I will seek the lost, and I will bring back the strayed, and I will bind up the crippled, and I will strengthen the weak, and the fat and the strong I will watch over; I will feed them in justice.

[17]"As for you, my flock, thus says the Lord GOD; Behold, I judge between one sheep and another, between sheep and goats. [23]And I will set up over them one shepherd, my servant David, and he shall feed them: he shall feed them and be their shepherd. [24]And I, the LORD, will be their God, and my servant David shall be chief among them; I, the LORD, have spoken."

SECOND READING

R 1 Corinthians 15:20–26, 28
E L 1 Corinthians 15:20–28

²⁰In fact Christ has been raised from the dead, the first fruits of those who have fallen asleep. For as by a human being came death, by a human being has come also the resurrection of the dead. For as in Adam all die, so also in Christ shall all be made alive. But each in the corresponding order: Christ the first fruits, then at his coming those who belong to Christ. Then comes the end, when Christ delivers the dominion to God, the Father, after destroying every rule and every authority and power. For Christ must reign until he has put all his enemies under his feet. ²⁶The last enemy to be destroyed is death. ²⁷For "God has put all things in subjection under the feet of him." But when it says, "All things are put in subjection under him," it is plain that the one is excepted who put all things under him. ²⁸When all things are subjected to Christ, then the Son himself will also be subjected to the one who put all things under him, that God may be everything to every one.

GOSPEL

R E L Matthew 25:31–46

[At that time Jesus said,]

³¹"When the Man of Heaven comes in his glory, and all the angels with him, then he will sit on his glorious throne. Before him will be gathered all the nations, and he will separate them one from another as a shepherd separates the sheep from the goats, and he will place the sheep at his right hand, but the goats at the left. Then the king will say to those at his right hand, 'Come, O blessed of my Father, inherit the realm prepared for you from the foundation of the world; for I was hungry and you gave me food, I was thirsty and you gave me drink, I was a stranger and you welcomed me, I was naked and you clothed me, I was sick and you visited me, I was in prison and you came to me.' Then the righteous will answer him, 'Lord, when did we see you hungry and feed you, or thirsty and give you drink? And when did we see you a

stranger and welcome you, or naked and clothe you? And when did we see you sick or in prison and visit you?' And the king will answer them, 'Truly, I say to you, as you did to one of the littlest of these my dear people, you did it to me.' Then the king will say to those at his left hand, 'Depart from me, you cursed, into the eternal fire prepared for the devil and the devil's angels; for I was hungry and you gave me no food, I was thirsty and you gave me no drink, I was a stranger and you did not welcome me, naked and you did not clothe me, sick and in prison and you did not visit me.' Then they also will answer, 'Lord, when did we see you hungry or thirsty or a stranger or naked or sick or in prison, and did not minister to you?' Then he will answer them, 'Truly, I say to you, as you did it not to one of the littlest of these, you did it not to me.' [46]And they will go away into eternal punishment, but the righteous into eternal life."

R E L   THE PRESENTATION OF THE LORD

FIRST READING

R E Malachi 3:1–4

¹"Behold, I send my messenger to prepare the way before me, and the Lord whom you seek will suddenly come to the temple; behold, the messenger of the covenant in whom you delight is coming, says the LORD of hosts. But who can endure the day of the messenger's coming, and who can stand when he appears?

"For he is like a refiner's fire and like fullers' soap; he will sit as a refiner and purifier of silver and will purify the Levites and refine them like gold and silver, till they present right offerings to the LORD. ⁴Then the offering of Judah and Jerusalem will be pleasing to the LORD as in the days of old and as in former years."

L 1 Samuel 1:21–28

²¹The man Elkanah and all his house went up to offer to the LORD the yearly sacrifice, and to pay his vow. But Hannah did not go up, for she said to her husband, "As soon as the child is weaned, I will bring him, that he may appear in the presence of the LORD, and abide there for ever." Elkanah her husband said to her, "Do what seems best to you, wait until you have weaned him; only, may the word of the LORD be established." So the woman remained and nursed her son, until she weaned him. And when she had weaned him, she took him up with her, along with a three-year-old bull, an ephah of flour, and a skin of wine; and she brought him to the house of the LORD at Shiloh; and the child was young. Then they slew the bull, and they brought the child to Eli. And Hannah said, "Oh, my lord! As you live, my lord, I am the woman who was standing here in your presence, praying to the LORD. For this child I prayed; and the LORD has granted me my petition which I made. ²⁸Therefore I have lent him to the LORD; as long as he lives, he is lent to the LORD."

SECOND READING

R E L Hebrews 2:14–18

14Since the children share in flesh and blood, Jesus himself likewise partook of the same nature, that through death he might
destroy the one who has the power of death, that is, the devil,
and deliver all those who through fear of death were subject to
lifelong bondage. For surely it is not with angels that Jesus is
concerned but with the descendants of Abraham. Therefore Jesus had to be made like his human family in every respect, so
that he might become a merciful and faithful high priest in the
service of God, to make expiation for the sins of the people.
18For because Jesus himself has suffered and been tempted, he
is able to help those who are tempted.

GOSPEL

R E L Luke 2:22–40

22When the time came for their purification according to the law
of Moses, they brought Jesus up to Jerusalem to present him to
the Lord (as it is written in the law of the Lord, "Every male
that opens the womb shall be called holy to the Lord") and to
offer a sacrifice according to what is said in the law of the Lord,
"a pair of turtledoves, or two young pigeons." Now there was
in Jerusalem a person named Simeon, who was righteous and
devout, looking for the consolation of Israel, and the Holy
Spirit was upon him. And it had been revealed to him by the
Holy Spirit that he should not see death before he had seen the
Lord's Christ. And inspired by the Spirit Simeon came into the
temple; and when the parents brought in the child Jesus, to do
for him according to the custom of the law, he took Jesus up in
his arms, and blessed God and said,

"Lord, now you let your servant go in peace;
your word has been fulfilled.
My own eyes have seen the salvation
which you have prepared in the sight of every people:
a light to reveal you to the nations
and the glory of your people Israel."

And his father and his mother marveled at what was said
about Jesus; and Simeon blessed them and said to Mary his
mother,
"Behold, this child is set for the fall and rising of many in
    Israel,
and for a sign that is spoken against
(and a sword will pierce through your own soul also),
that thoughts out of many hearts may be revealed."

And there was a prophetess, Anna, the daughter of Phanuel,
of the tribe of Asher; she was of a great age, having lived with
her husband seven years from her marriage, and as a widow
till she was eighty-four. She did not depart from the temple,
worshiping with fasting and prayer night and day. And coming
up at that very hour she gave thanks to God, and spoke of the
child to all who were looking for the redemption of Jerusalem.

And when the parents had performed everything according to
the law of the Lord, they returned into Galilee, to their own
city, Nazareth. ⁴⁰And the child grew and became strong, filled
with wisdom; and the favor of God was upon him.

R ASSUMPTION OF THE BLESSED VIRGIN MARY
E ST. MARY THE VIRGIN
L MARY, THE MOTHER OF OUR LORD

FIRST READING

R Revelation 11: 19, 12:1–6, 10ab

[19]Then God's temple in heaven was opened, and the ark of God's covenant was seen within God's temple; and there were flashes of lightning, voices, peals of thunder, an earthquake, and heavy hail.

[1]And a great portent appeared in heaven, a woman clothed with the sun, with the moon under her feet, and on her head a crown of twelve stars; she was with child and she cried out in her pangs of birth, in anguish for delivery. And another portent appeared in heaven; behold, a great red dragon, with seven heads and ten horns, and seven diadems upon its heads. Its tail swept down a third of the stars of heaven, and cast them to the earth. And the dragon stood before the woman who was about to bear a child, that it might devour her child when she brought it forth; she brought forth a male child, one who is to rule all the nations with a rod of iron, but her child was caught up to God and to God's throne, [6]and the woman fled into the wilderness, where she has a place prepared by God, in which to be nourished for one thousand two hundred and sixty days.

[10a]And I heard a loud voice in heaven, [10b]saying, "Now the salvation and the power and the dominion of our God and the authority of God's Christ have come."

E Isaiah 61:10–11
L Isaiah 61:7–11

[7]Instead of your shame you shall have a double portion,
  instead of dishonor you shall rejoice in your lot;
therefore in your land you shall possess a double portion;
  yours shall be everlasting joy.

For I the L$_{ORD}$ love justice,
  I hate robbery and wrong;
I will faithfully give them their recompense,
  and I will make an everlasting covenant with them.
Their descendants shall be known among the nations,
  and their offspring in the midst of the peoples;
all who see them shall acknowledge them,
  that they are a people whom the L$_{ORD}$ has blessed.
¹⁰I will greatly rejoice in the L$_{ORD}$,
  my soul shall exult in my God;
for God has clothed me with the garments of salvation,
  and covered me with the robe of righteousness,
as a bridegroom decks himself with a garland,
  and as a bride adorns herself with her jewels.
¹¹For as the earth brings forth its shoots,
  and as a garden causes what is sown in it to spring up,
so the Lord G$_{OD}$ will cause righteousness and praise
  to spring forth before all the nations.

SECOND READING

R   1 Corinthians 15:20–26

²⁰In fact Christ has been raised from the dead, the first fruits of
those who have fallen asleep. For as by a human being came
death, by a human being has come also the resurrection of the
dead. For as in Adam all die, so also in Christ shall all be made
alive. But each in the corresponding order: Christ the first
fruits, then at his coming those who belong to Christ. Then
comes the end, when Christ delivers the dominion to God, the
Father, after destroying every rule and every authority and
power. For Christ must reign until he has put all his enemies
under his feet. ²⁶The last enemy to be destroyed is death.

E   L   Galatians 4:4–7

⁴When the time had fully come, God sent forth the Son, born
of woman, born under the law, to redeem those who were
under the law, so that we might receive adoption. And because
you are adopted children, God has sent the Spirit of the Son
into our hearts, crying, "Abba! Father!" ⁷So through God you

are no longer a slave but an adopted child, and if a child then
an heir.

GOSPEL

R   Luke 1:39–56
E L   Luke 1:46–55

³⁹In those days Mary arose and went with haste into the hill
country, to a city of Judah, and she entered the house of Zechariah and greeted Elizabeth. And when Elizabeth heard the
greeting of Mary, the baby leaped in her womb; and Elizabeth
was filled with the Holy Spirit and she exclaimed with a loud
cry, "Blessed are you among women, and blessed is the fruit of
your womb! And why is this granted me, that the mother of
my Lord should come to me? For behold, when the voice of
your greeting came to my ears, the baby in my womb leaped
for joy. And blessed is she who believed that there would be a
fulfillment of what was spoken to her from the Lord." ⁴⁶And
Mary said,

"My soul magnifies the Lord,
and my spirit rejoices in God my Savior
who has looked with favor on me, a lowly serving maid.
From this day all generations will call me blessed.
The Mighty One has done great things for me;
holy the name of the Lord,
whose mercy is on the God-fearing
from generation to generation.
The arm of the Lord is filled with strength,
scattering the proudhearted.
God hurled the mighty from their thrones,
lifting up the lowly.
God filled the hungry with good things,
sending the rich away empty.
God has come to the help of Israel, the Lord's servant,
remembering mercy,
⁵⁵the mercy promised to our forebears,
to Abraham and his children forever."

⁵⁶And Mary remained with her about three months, and re-
turned to her home.

SCRIPTURAL INDEX